Vassar College

THE CAMPUS GUIDE

Vassar College

AN ARCHITECTURAL TOUR BY

Karen Van Lengen and Lisa Reilly

PHOTOGRAPHS BY

Will Faller

FOREWORD BY

Frances D. Fergusson

Princeton Architectural Press

NEW YORK | *2004*

Princeton Architectural Press
37 East Seventh Street
New York, New York 10003

For a free catalog of books, call 1.800.722.6657.
Visit our web site at www.papress.com.

Photograph on page 28 © Stephen Leek.

Series editor: Jan Cigliano
Series concept: Dennis Looney
Project editor: Nicola Bednarek
Layout: Mary-Neal Meador
Maps: Jane Sheinman

Special thanks to: Nettie Aljian, Janet Behning, Megan Carey, Penny (Yuen Pik) Chu,
Russell Fernandez, Jan Haux, Clare Jacobson, Mark Lamster, Nancy Eklund Later, Linda
Lee, Katharine Myers, Scott Tennent, Jennifer Thompson, Joseph Weston, and Deb
Wood of Princeton Architectural Press —Kevin C. Lippert, publisher

Library of Congress Cataloging-in-Publication Data

Van Lengen, Karen.
  Vassar College / Karen Van Lengen and Lisa Reilly ; photographs by
Will Faller ; foreword by Frances D. Fergusson.—1st ed.
    p. cm. — (The campus guide)
Includes bibliographical references and index.
  ISBN 1-56898-349-2 (alk. paper)
 1. Vassar College—Buildings—Guidebooks. 2. Vassar College—History.
3. Vassar College—Pictorial works. I. Reilly, Lisa A. II. Faller,
Will. III. Title. IV. Campus guide (New York, N.Y.)
  LD7184 .V36 2004
  378.747'33—dc21
                                    2002006002

Printed in Hong Kong

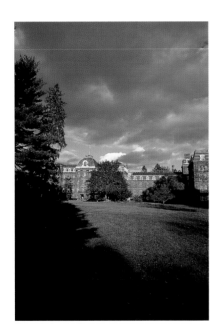

This book is intended for visitors, alumnae/i, and students who wish to have an insider's look at the Vassar campus, from James Renwick, Jr.'s, Main Building of 1865, to Marcel Breuer's 1951 Ferry House, to Cesar Pelli's Frances Lehman Loeb Art Center of 1994.

The guide opens with an introduction that charts the chronological development of the Vassar campus, reflecting the college's institutional history. Vassar's architectural evolution is thus understood in relation to contemporary ideas about women's education and the college's transformation into a fully coeducational liberal arts college. The introduction is followed by an essay that analyzes the rich landscape architecture of the Vassar campus, which has been a defining feature of its character throughout the college's history. The book is arranged around one continuous walk, presented here in four chapters, that leads the reader around the campus with informative profiles and photographs of each building or site. A three-dimensional map identifies the buildings on the walk.

Visitors are welcome to tour the Vassar campus:
Please check in at the Main Gate, where you will receive a visitor's parking pass and campus map. A map of the arboretum is also available.

Public Tours: Office of College Relations, Main Building, second floor north, 124 Raymond Avenue, Poughkeepsie, New York 12604, (845) 437 7400

Prospective Student Tours: Office of Admissions, Carol and James Kautz Admission House, (845) 437 7300, http://admissions.vassar.edu

Frances Lehman Loeb Art Center: Open to the public, free admission. Tuesday–Saturday, 10 am–5 pm; Sunday 1–5 pm. For group tours call (845) 437 7745; http://fflac.vassar.edu

Vassar College Libraries: http://library.vassar.edu

Class of 1951 Observatory: Open to the public at selected times; for information call (845) 437 7340

Arches, Blodgett Hall

Lisa Reilly (Vassar 1978) and Karen Van Lengen (Vassar 1973) wrote this book collaboratively. The introductory essay *Introduction to Vassar College* is by Reilly with contributions from Van Lengen for the post–World War II history of the college. The second essay, *From Racetrack to Academic Park: The Legacy of the Landscape*, was written by Van Lengen. The entries for buildings constructed through the presidency of Henry MacCracken, which ended in 1946, are by Reilly. Van Lengen is the author of the entries for landscape features and buildings constructed from 1946 to the present with the exception of the entry on the new Center for Drama and Film by Cesar Pelli and Associates, which was written by Julia Van Develder.

We would like to thank Jennifer Lathrop, a graduate student in architectural history and architecture at the University of Virginia who has provided research and editorial assistance of the finest quality. Eric Field and K. C. Squires, of the University of Virginia, provided assistance in creating the diagrams of the campus plans included in the two introductory essays. Richard Guy Wilson, Commonwealth Professor at the University of Virginia, generously shared his vast knowledge of American architecture with us. We also thank Brenda Korfanty and Patty deCourcy for their administrative support during this project.

We wish to thank President Frances D. Fergusson for her generous support of this book. We thank Jeh Johnson, professor of architecture at Vassar from 1965–2001, for his guidance and mentorship. The Special Collections Library, headed by Ron Patkus, was a huge resource for this book. We extend our gratitude to Dean Rogers in Special Collections, who, with great humor and efficiency, diligently supported our research through its evolution. We thank John McEnrue, a project manager for buildings and grounds at Vassar, who enthusiastically provided maps, information, and assistance in locating architectural documentation as well as helping us to understand recent renovations and additions to the campus. Thanks also go to Christy Drinkard, his assistant, for her kind help.

We are also greatly indebted to Elizabeth Daniels, Vassar Professor Emeritus of English and Vassar historian, who identified a wealth of resources on the history of the college and its buildings. Her publications about Vassar provided a starting point for this project.

We would also like to thank Robert Pounder, special assistant to the president; Joann Potter, registrar and collections manager, and Patricia Phagan, curator of prints and drawings, both of the Frances Lehman Loeb Art Center; John Mihaly, director of regional programs in the Vassar development office; Susan DeKrey, vice president for college relations; and her executive assistant, Susan Kowalski, for their assistance on this project. Vassar College would also like to thank Julia Van Develder, editorial director in the office of college relations.

We thank Nicola Bednarek from Princeton Architectural Press for her conscientious editing, Jane Sheinman for her maps, and Will Faller for his excellent photography.

Karen Van Lengen and Lisa Reilly
Charlottesville, 2003

Library lawn, with view of Rockefeller Hall

Foreword

The architecture of Vassar is brilliantly eclectic, a true omnium-gatherum of advanced and fashionable architectural styles from the college's founding in 1861 to the present day. Matthew Vassar brought money, brains, and enthusiasm for the arts to his new college. He early proclaimed his determination to do "all things intellectual and material the best."[1] Vassar lived by that dictum, hiring the protean James Renwick, Jr., to build his college, the Main Building of our present day. As Karen Van Lengen and Lisa Reilly so deftly demonstrate, Vassar presidents have followed Matthew Vassar's example, adding notably over the decades to the architectural pleasures of this extraordinary campus. Those additions have been bold, inventive, often large in scale, and varied in style. The result is one of the most beautiful, and most interesting, campuses one might imagine.

Other campuses have often adopted an official, repetitive college style, generally Georgian or Gothic. Vassar, in the college's determination to be always of its time, gave much more stylistic freedom to its architects, asking only that they produce their best. Occasionally eyebrows rose, and typically energetic Vassar discussion ensued. In a less ordered world, the architectural result could be disharmonious, perhaps even chaotic. At Vassar, however, the landscape mediates and establishes the context for each building and its relation to the next. Green spaces have had as much prominence in planning as the buildings. With rare exceptions, Vassar has known where not to build buildings, protecting the open spaces, the verdant views, the bordered quadrangles and circles, the special orbit of each structure and its place within the whole.

Indeed, concurrent with the development of its built environment, Vassar developed an arboretum of significance, with over two hundred varieties of trees, whose scale and magnificence rival that of the architecture.

The Vassar Quadrangle

Campus lawn, with view of Maria Mitchell Observatory

Vassar thus has an arboretum of trees combined with an "*edificeum*" of buildings, working together to create a singularly deft and varied visual complex. Those who explore the Vassar campus leave with impressions of its weighty splendor, as well as its special visual surprises. The campus has both grandeur and small niches and sites for solitude and contemplation.

There is at Vassar a strong sense of place that affects all who come to know her. In later life, our alumni discover the campus etched in their mind's eye with clarity and affection. In a world in which so much changes with such rapidity, the college offers reassuring continuity. For those who return to Vassar—whether after ten years or seventy years—the campus remains comfortingly familiar. Both buildings and landscapes have been carefully preserved and restored, and new interventions reflect a continuing visual dialog with the ideas and the ideal of the campus. This is a campus where planning guides the shape of what happens, where new architecture, however bold, takes its place within a larger context of buildings and nature, carefully ordered.

Frances D. Fergusson
President, Vassar College

Introduction

The main gate of Vassar College opens onto one of the great vistas of American campus architecture. Main Building, James Renwick, Jr.'s, elegant masterpiece, stands today on axis with the gatehouse and dominates the entrance to the college just as it did when Vassar opened in 1865. The wide sweep of lawns to the right and left of the entrance drive is bordered by the exquisite architectural diversity of Vassar's art gallery, chapel, President's House, classroom buildings, and library. The mature plantings and gardens, planned from the college's beginning, were recently renovated under current president Frances D. Fergusson, who, like her predecessors, recognized the importance of the environment for educational institutions. Vassar's nineteenth-century founders carefully considered how to establish the setting for a new type of institution: a college for women. They realized the importance of architectural form and landscape as emblems of the college as well as their role in shaping the experience of students and faculty.

The story of Vassar's development from the first college for women into one of today's premier coeducational institutions can be told through the rich architectural history of the campus.[1] At its entrance, the original Second Empire–style Main Building by Renwick is balanced by the magnificent early twentieth-century Gothic revival gatehouse and library opposite. Two of the most recent additions to the campus, Cesar Pelli's Frances Lehman Loeb Art Center and Hardy Holzman Pfeiffer's Martha Rivers and E. Bronson Ingram Library addition, complete the framing of the great lawn.

Main Building, 1872

Aerial Photo of Main Campus (ca. 2000)

Vassar's campus did not emerge out of a single overall design, as was the case at such universities as Stanford or Rice. Rather, the campus unfolded, sometimes in sections, under the direction of its founder Matthew Vassar along with a series of visionary presidents. These leaders developed the campus as an articulation of the college's evolving educational mission and identity. In keeping with the strong sense of uniqueness and diversity that has always been part of Vassar's identity, the college architecture today does not adhere to one dominant style but features exquisite examples of many styles, including medieval revival, Second Empire, colonial revival, beaux arts, high modernism, and postmodern representatives. The campus architecture thus charts the history of collegiate education in America. From its founding as the first college for women to its preeminent position in coeducation today, Vassar has been a pioneer in the evolution of American higher education.

The Vassar, Jewett, and Raymond Years, 1861–78

> "If you will establish a real college for girls and endow it, you will build a monument for yourself more lasting than the pyramids."[2]
>
> —Milo Jewett, educator

As the childless Matthew Vassar, a self-made millionaire who amassed his fortune through his brewing company, neared the end of his life, he wished to found a philanthropic institution to preserve his name. He originally

Portrait of Matthew Vassar by Charles Loring Elliott, 1861

considered establishing a hospital on the model of a relative who had endowed Guy's Hospital in London but educator Milo Jewett, later the first president of Vassar College, convinced Vassar to break with convention and found the first college for women as his monument to posterity. Jewett was an experienced educator from Alabama who purchased from the wealthy Poughkeepsie brewer in 1855 a local girls' school known as Cottage Hill Seminary, formerly run by Vassar's late niece, Lydia Booth. Discussions with Lydia Booth had already spurred Vassar's interest in greater educational opportunities for women, as his papers record, and he was soon intrigued by Jewett's idea.[3] Once convinced that founding the first women's college would be a worthy memorial to himself and a deserving philanthropic goal, Vassar pursued the project with characteristic energy and enthusiasm. In 1859 he selected a site for the future college approximately three miles east of Poughkeepsie.[4] In January of 1861, Vassar Female College received a charter from the New York State Legislature, and in February, the trustees elected Jewett the first president of the college.[5] On February 26, 1861, Vassar presented an endowment of over $400, 000 and the deed to two hundred acres to the new college's trustees at their first meeting.[6] Although later eroded by the financial instabilities caused by the Civil War, Vassar's gift was originally considered more than adequate for his purpose. As the college became his life's work, Vassar continued to add to his original gift as the need arose.

From the beginning, Vassar and Jewett realized the importance of architecture as a metaphor for the new educational venture the college represented. While education for women was not new, a college education on a par with that available to men was. Vassar wanted the intellectual excellence of his new institution to be apparent through its built form while also offering reassurance to a society uncomfortable with the idea of female equality and independence. Being aware of the progressive nature of their proposal, Vassar and Jewett sought a suitable architectural form to house their innovative institution.

In 1862 Jewett traveled abroad to study educational institutions while Vassar continued to develop the program and buildings for the new campus.[7] Vassar was personally involved in every aspect of the college's design—sometimes to the frustration of Jewett and the board of trustees. In his letters, diaries, and remarks at trustees' meetings, Vassar expressed concern about the safety and purity of the water supply, the effectiveness of the heating system, daily progress of the building construction, and curricular issues as well as his sense of the magnitude of his undertaking. In some notes jotted down at the end of his diary of 1864, Vassar wrote, "The founder of Vassar College and President Lincoln—Two Noble Emancipists—one of Woman—the [other of the] Negro—."[8] While this claim may seem overstated today, Vassar's letters and diaries clearly reveal an intention to move well beyond the status quo in women's education. His famous remark of his intention "to build and endow a college for young women which shall be to them what Yale and Harvard are to young men" is revealing. He had come to view women as men's intellectual equals and wanted to provide a physical plant for his college that was as impressive as that found at Harvard. He did not wish to follow the modest path of the female seminary observed at Mount Holyoke. This clearly shows that even though Vassar did put forward the traditional view that women should be well educated because of their critical social role as mothers and educators of their children, he also advocated wider opportunities for women after college. These conflicting goals reemerge in various ways throughout Vassar's history. The early college's faculty, curriculum, and academic facilities, for example, would proclaim the sincerity of Matthew Vassar's intention to revolutionize women's education whereas the college's regulations and residential arrangements suggested his compliance with traditional social limits on women's behavior.

Considering a female faculty necessary as role models for the students, Matthew Vassar in fact wanted women professors for his new college, stating in February of 1864, "Let us prove the certainty of woman's higher possible future by the best examples from the present. Let us recognize and honor her existing talent first." During a trustees' discussion of faculty hires in June 1864, Vassar said:

> I wish to give one sex all the advantages too long monopolized by the other. Ours is, and is to be, an institution for women—not men.... This, I conceive may be fully accomplished within the rational limits of true womanliness, and without the slightest hazard to the attractiveness of her character.... We are defeated if we start upon the assumption that she has no powers, save those she may derive or imitate from the other sex.... We are especially defeated if we fail to express by our acts our practical belief in her pre-eminent powers as an instructor of her own sex.[9]

The trustees, however, generally felt that a faculty of women would diminish the college's intended reputation as a female rival to Harvard and Yale, since they would not be as well-trained or distinguished as a male faculty. In the end, Vassar found his aim of an all-female faculty difficult to realize as few women were qualified for positions as professors in the 1860s. In an early instance of academic headhunting, however, the world-renowned astronomer Maria Mitchell was successfully wooed by the Vassar trustees and became one of two female members of the college's original faculty, together with physician and physiology professor Alida C. Avery.[10]

Another challenge Vassar faced was the fact that he could not build upon any previous models for the development of his college's campus. Although the curriculum, faculty, and facilities could follow those at Harvard and Yale, the college's physical plant, with its need to provide young women with an appropriate domestic environment, could not. While Princeton's multipurpose Nassau Hall of 1784 was a popular prototype for late-eighteenth- and early nineteenth-century American college buildings, by the 1860s, men's colleges typically used separate buildings for different types of activities.[11] The largely independent lifestyles of male college students housed in a scattering of small dormitories without close supervision, as seen at the University of Virginia, for example, would not have been possible for a women's institution of the 1860s. In order for the new college to succeed, Vassar had to house his radical education program in a setting recognized as familiar and secure by his potential students and their families.[12] Hence, although drawing on the curricula of Harvard and Yale, he studied the building types of women's seminaries such as Mount Holyoke.

The seminary model, which relied on the plan of a house, featured a main entrance that opened into a series of public rooms. Unlike the dormitories of contemporary men's institutions, bedrooms were housed in more private parts of the building rather than opening off a staircase or entryway accessible from the exterior of the building.[13] This expanded domestic dwelling also followed the hierarchical ordering of the seminary in reinforcing the separation of students and teachers as well as the organization of faculty by rank in classroom arrangements, dining room seating, and the disposition of public rooms.[14] Sarah Hale, an early advocate for the college, was clear about the need for a domestic setting for women students:

> It is plain that the independence which young men may, in a college life, enjoy without injury, would be pernicious to young girls.... *The home life* is an essential element in woman's education, necessary for the best development of her mind and the perfection of her character.

Rendering of Renwick's design for Vassar Female College (1864)

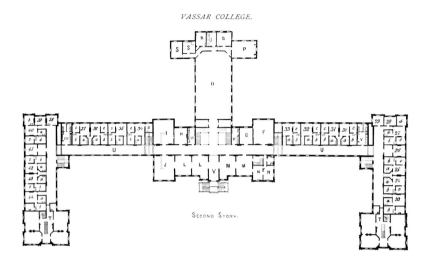

Plan of second story of Main Building, from B. Lossing, Vassar College and Its Founder, *1876.*

> Therefore, the plan of making this collegiate institution a pleasant
> HOME, for all who are educated under its privileges, was wise and
> beneficent.[15]

In contrast to Mount Holyoke's original building, famously characterized as
"plain but very neat," Matthew Vassar's main building proclaimed his larger
vision for his college. Drawing on the grand architectural traditions of
Europe, Renwick's building, the largest in the United States at the time, was
clearly ambitious and indeed became *the* model for future women's colleges
both in the U.S. and abroad.[16] While Main's grand facade and elegant public
rooms were distinctly different from the plain simplicity of Mount Holyoke,
its interior spatial organization similarly aimed at permitting the close supervision of young women away from home, which was so important to contemporary society. In a letter to Reverend Rufus Babcock on October 23,
1861, Vassar wrote: "What I regard as an essential element of our Institution
is the perfect *Control* of the pupils during the period of their instruction in
the College, anything short of this is a yielding up of our immediate
guardianship while the responsibility remains."[17] Main's architectural program was clearly intended to support this goal.

   After years of planning, Vassar Female College opened its doors on
September 20, 1865, to 353 students ranging in age from fourteen to twenty-
four and coming from twenty-two different states and the kingdom of
Hawaii. The plan of the original campus shows a small cluster of buildings
standing at the center of the 198-acre site. The first participants in Vassar's

Southeast view of Avery Hall from Sunset Hill, c. 1870

pioneering enterprise passed through the college's gate to find the new campus dominated, then as now, by Renwick's Main Building. Early engravings suggest a parklike setting with formal gardens appropriate to the Second Empire vocabulary of Main flanking the building and a more naturalized, picturesque landscape beyond. Actual photographs from the early days of the college show a plainer, less articulated landscape.

Behind Main stood three smaller subsidiary structures whose functions tell much about the founder's intention for his institution. Matthew Vassar was particularly keen to provide a safe and hygienic home for the college community as well as a place outfitted with the most modern equipment available. Discreetly tucked behind Main was a power plant, which used the most modern technology available to provide steam heat and lighting for the campus. The observatory, one of the best equipped in the nation, stood on a small hill about eight hundred feet northeast of the Main Building. To the southeast of Main stood the Calisthenium and Riding Academy Building, which opened in the college's second year, later known as Avery Hall, and now transformed into the new Center for Drama and Film. The building had outstanding facilities and was described by the *New York Times* as the most beautiful in this country, second only to those at West Point.[18] In addition to the high academic standards Matthew Vassar set for his college, he also wanted to provide for adequate physical exercise for his students, being aware

Maria Mitchell with her assistant Mary Whitney in the observatory, c. 1888

of the claim that women's physical weakness rendered them unsuited to the strains of serious academic study. An innovative program of daily physical exercise was incorporated into the college's curriculum. While the riding program was closed for financial reasons less than ten years after the college opened, the program of individualized physical education housed in the Calisthenium became an enduring part of the college's curriculum. This core of buildings was augmented by the landscape feature known as the Circle on Main's east side, which provided further room for exercise and botanical study.

The lavish, well-equipped campus reflected years of planning by both the college founder, Matthew Vassar, and its first president, Milo P. Jewett. Relations between the founder, the trustees, and President Jewett had

Avery Hall, nineteenth century

grown tense, however, as the college's opening day neared, and in spring of 1864, Jewett resigned as president, following a break with Matthew Vassar. Jewett thus never presided over the students whose college he had worked for nearly ten years to shape. John Raymond (1864–78), member of the board of trustees and "an educator of long experience," replaced the man who had given Vassar the vision for his college.[19]

Under its second president, the college continued to mediate between offering women advanced educational opportunities and abiding by social conventions. In a report prepared at the request of the United States Commissioner of Education, Raymond outlined the college's administrative organization:

> The internal organization has two branches, educational and domestic.... Domestic arrangements have of late been regarded in this country as of doubtful utility in colleges for young men; but the Founder and the Board of Trustees deemed them indispensable, for the present at least, in a college for young women. The plan of the buildings and the organization of the college have been adjusted to this view.[20]

Raymond defined his presidential role as being an overseer of the interests of the college, ensuring its adherence to outside regulations, and serving as a guardian of the students' religious and moral instruction. He identified the lady principal as his chief executive aide and immediate head of the college family, who "exercises a maternal supervision over the deportment, health, social connections, personal habits, and wants of the students."[21]

Vassar had hired Hannah Lyman as lady principal, a position second only to that of the college president, to enforce high standards of behavior among the students. Lyman herself had been educated under the seminary system, which was marked by close supervision and a highly regulated daily schedule. Lyman was particularly concerned with ladylike dress for her charges and shunned the emphasis on plain clothing and domestic duties that was part of the Mount Holyoke system. She required Vassar students to change before dinner and personally measured their dress lengths.

Young women teachers who taught academic subjects under the supervision of the professorial faculty oversaw the personal lives of their students under Lyman's direction. Study time, room tidiness, and bath schedules were all overseen by these women, who were known as corridor mistresses and whose own lives were in turn controlled by Lyman herself. From the beginning, this regulated life was challenged by Maria Mitchell, as well as some of her male colleagues.[22] The contrast between Mitchell, with her emphasis on intellectual achievement, and Lyman's goal of ladylike deportment, represented the dichotomy of women's collegiate education in the nineteenth century. A profile of Vassar College written at the time of its centennial in 1961 discussed Mitchell and Lyman, noting that these "two figures, the feminist and the lady, stood for two currents that flowed side by side through Vassar."[23] Vassar students themselves, unlike their Mount Holyoke contemporaries, were unwilling participants in Lyman's highly regulated life and defied her system both openly and secretly. They used the eccentricities of Main's residential quarters, which featured suites of rooms that did not open directly onto the corridors, to avoid surveillance by Lyman and her corridor mistresses. In fact, the building so carefully planned to allow close supervision of its student residents inadvertently provided them with many opportunities for clandestine activities.[24] Helen Horowitz suggests that the diversity of Vassar's student body in terms of age and background set it apart from other women's institutions and may have been responsible for the independent spirit of the Vassar woman from the start.[25]

As Vassar College charted unknown territory in its early years, it became known for the success of its high-quality education. Restricting the behavior of its pioneering students proved difficult, however. In the text of the speech the founder was about to give at the time of his death he noted, "If we only follow on in the old beaten paths we will make no progress. We do no more than others have done before us. We are only copyists and not progressionists. My motto is progress."[26]

Main Annex, known as "Uncle Fred's Nose," constructed in 1893 to house the library; destroyed in 1959

The Caldwell and Taylor Years, 1878–1914

Vassar's unique offerings as the only institution of its kind for women guaranteed its success for its first years of operation. By 1875, with the opening of Smith and Wellesley along with Mount Holyoke's eventual transformation into a collegiate institution, Vassar faced stiff competition. These difficulties were exacerbated by the unexpected death of President Raymond and the rapid appointment of an ill-qualified successor, Samuel Caldwell (1878–85). During Caldwell's brief presidency, the college experienced a period of tremendous uncertainty. In his history of Vassar, James Monroe Taylor, Vassar's fourth president (1886–1914), articulated the reasons behind the college's difficulties during Caldwell's tenure.[27] Taylor acknowledged the financial problems caused by the need to keep the college at full enrollment in

James Monroe Taylor, Vassar's fourth president (1886–1914)

order to maintain an enormous building like Main. He also mentioned Vassar's higher tuition, the rigidity of its admission policy, and its growing reputation as a prep school rather than a college due to the size of its own preparatory department. The college was already facing an enrollment crisis by the time of Caldwell's appointment with only 171 out of the total 306 students enrolled in Vassar's college program.[28] The remaining 135 were chiefly enrolled in a preparatory program the college had developed under President Raymond in recognition of the fact that many of its eager and able applicants were not adequately prepared for a rigorous collegiate curriculum.[29] Some were enrolled in special, non-degree programs in music or art.

The one bright spot in Caldwell's presidency was the construction of the Vassar Brothers Laboratory of Chemistry and Physics in 1880, the first new building since the college opened. With this addition, Vassar signaled its intention to continue as a collegiate institution with the most modern of science facilities. As enrollments continued to decline, however, Caldwell was forced to resign as president in 1885 in response to alumnae criticisms of his administration.[30]

Taylor became president in 1886, and, in his history of Vassar College, he entitled the chapter on his presidency "The Period of Expansion" in stark contrast to the chapter about Caldwell, which was called "The Period of Discouragement."[31] In closing the preparatory department, Taylor thus risked the college's financial security rather than lose Vassar's reputation as a collegiate institution forever. Taylor thus refocused the college once again on its primary mission of providing a collegiate education for women and responded to the challenge of its more recently founded rivals.

By the time of Taylor's presidency, Vassar's buildings looked outdated and its facilities were no longer keeping pace with institutions like Smith and Wellesley.[32] These colleges offered cottage-style residential quarters—smaller, more homelike living quarters than Main's lengthy corridors.[33] In addition, Vassar's facilities for physical education and science and the library were no longer adequate, and its academic program required updating and regularizing. By this time, Wellesley's campus included a music building, art building and museum, as well as the residential cottages.[34]

President Taylor met the challenge of such modern competition and gave visible form to Vassar's revitalization by expanding the college facilities. Taylor also made clear Vassar's continuing presence as a serious institution of higher learning through his revision of the college's curriculum and restructuring of its administration.[35] Vassar's second great period of building began as Taylor successfully attracted donations from major philanthropists such as John D. Rockefeller.

Taylor's building program followed the examples of Smith and Wellesley by extending the campus beyond the core of structures clustered around Main, and by developing two other principal areas of building, one primarily academic and the other chiefly residential. His success in refocusing Vassar on its collegiate mission led to the need for new residential facilities as it brought about an increase in enrollment that outstripped the college's available housing facilities. Many students were obliged to live in boarding houses in Poughkeepsie, where it was difficult for the college to guarantee adequate facilities. In order to accommodate the growing number of students as well as offer housing equal to that of its rivals, a residential precinct was developed to the north of Main Building, beginning with the construction of Strong Residential Hall in 1893. Work continued with the formation of a quadrangle through the construction of Raymond (1897), Lathrop (1901), and Davison (1902). Jewett House, originally known as

Renwick's Gatehouse at Raymond Avenue

North Tower, completed the ensemble in 1907, with Josselyn added to the housing stock in 1912. This expansion enabled the college to once again become a truly residential community. In addition to upgrading student accommodations, Taylor also developed housing for faculty across Raymond Avenue, which offered them greater privacy and independence.

At the same time, the academic side of the campus underwent major transformations as the college sought to upgrade its facilities. With his additions of New England Building (1901) and Sanders Classroom (1909), Taylor established a center for the sciences on the south side of Main. The alumnae provided considerable support in this great expansion, donating the New England Building and Alumnae Gymnasium (1889). Rockefeller Hall (1897) provided relief for the overcrowded classrooms. The perimeter of the great lawns in front of Main was now defined by this new composition of building types—a classroom building, a library, a chapel, and the President's House—as the many facilities once housed in Main moved to larger, more modern buildings. Main was no longer the only building visible from the gateway, although its dominance of the campus was assured by the decision to keep the lawns in front of it clear of further development. For the first time, the college had a campus of substantial buildings spreading out across the landscape where Vassar had laid out his gardens and walkways.

Two eminent architectural firms designed over half of these buildings: Allen & Collens and York & Sawyer. Allen & Collens served as the college's consulting architects designing twelve buildings at Vassar (including five of MacCracken's projects).[36] The association began when Francis Allen designed Strong House in 1893 and continued when he and Charles Collens became partners in 1904. After Allen's death in 1931, Collens continued as consulting architect at Vassar until 1937. Boston-based, the firm built a large number of well-known monuments including Riverside Church in New York; Brown Tower, James Tower, and the Memorial Chapel at Union Theological Seminary; and eight buildings at Williams College. Although their buildings show a variety of styles, Allen and Collens are best known as Gothic revival architects, as their work at Vassar suggests.

York & Sawyer began its celebrated partnership with the design of Rockefeller Hall in 1897.[37] From this project, it became one of the most distinguished firms of its day and went on to design seven more buildings at Vassar—three under President Taylor and four under his successor Henry Noble MacCracken. York & Sawyer employed a medieval revival vocabulary for four of its buildings at Vassar, and between the two firms, medieval revival was established as the dominant style of the campus. York & Sawyer also designed two colonial revival buildings as well as a beaux-arts structure for the campus. Vassar's medieval revival buildings are drawn from a variety of sources, ranging from Romanesque to Gothic to Tudor. Built out of a wide range of materials, they do not form a unified group, and all of them

Vassar Chapel, c. 1907

contrast with the Second Empire–style of Renwick's Main Building. Thus, Taylor's presidency established a tradition of diversity for the development of Vassar's architecture.

Taylor's gamble of returning Vassar to its original purpose succeeded. Enrollment grew to about one thousand students during his presidency as the college regained its reputation for excellence. While Taylor initiated a modernization of the college's campus and curriculum, a patriarchal attitude toward students and faculty persisted at Vassar as at other women's colleges.[38] Taylor and his trustees tried to create an institution sheltered from the world at large, preparing students for a life of academic pursuits. By the time of his retirement in 1914, Vassar's faculty was eager to take on a greater role in the college's decision-making process, while students sought engagement with contemporary issues such as women's suffrage as well as relief from Vassar's restrictive social regulations.[39] Taylor would not allow the issue of women's suffrage to be debated at Vassar, refusing to let Jane Addams speak at the college as a representative of the Collegiate League for Equal Suffrage.[40]

While he maintained his stand against progressive social issues, however, faculty such as Lucy Maynard Salmon and Herbert Mills, following in the footsteps of Maria Mitchell, were educating students to become independent thinkers who questioned conventional views. When Taylor banned a women's suffrage meeting in 1912, the students moved the gathering to a nearby cemetery beyond his control.[41] Through his construction of over twenty buildings designed by the leading architects of his day, Taylor had modernized Vassar's campus but not his thinking about women's role in society. His successor, Henry Noble MacCracken, would bring Vassar into the modern era with new ideas about women's education and its relevance to the world beyond Vassar's gates.

The MacCracken Years, 1915–46

Henry Noble MacCracken, a thirty-four-year-old energetic professor of medieval literature, was inaugurated as Vassar's fifth president in 1915.[42] For thirty-one years thereafter he steered the college on a course of academic leadership with an emphasis on individual responsibility and the importance of public service. MacCracken was a social activist who sought to preserve Vassar's pioneering spirit. Upon his resignation in 1946, the trustees noted: "Under your leadership, Vassar has never been an ivory tower, but has been constantly sensitive to the rapidly changing world of the past thirty years. You have kept vigorously before your students an ideal of learning for social usefulness."[43] MacCracken encouraged autonomy on the part of the faculty and students through a revision of the college's rules and administrative structure. These self-governance procedures, which served as a model for colleges across the country, gave students in particular greater control over their own lives and were in stark contrast to the highly regulated life the first Vassar students had known under Lady Principal Hannah Lyman.[44]

As MacCracken encouraged greater independence among all facets of the Vassar community, he also strove to broaden the college's horizon by hosting conferences and speakers on a wide range of issues. His desire to develop Vassar's reputation as a center for innovation as well as academic excellence found further expression in his curricular reforms.[45] MacCracken wanted to maintain the college's traditional emphasis on the liberal arts while also opening up the curriculum to new programs that would equip its students to take on leadership roles as new opportunities emerged, particularly for work in the area of public welfare.[46] His architectural program at Vassar, which includes some of the campus's most beautiful buildings such as Cushing House and Skinner and Blodgett halls, addressed both the traditional and innovative aspects of his curricular developments. Under MacCracken, Vassar continued to rely on the eminent firms of Allen & Collens, and York & Sawyer. Skinner Hall provided a first-rate facility for the continuing development of the college's premier music program, while Kendrick House offered further opportunities for more independent living arrangements for female faculty members off campus. These two were designed in a medieval revival style, popular throughout college campuses in the early twentieth century. Although he had sanctioned mostly traditional building styles, in his later years, MacCracken reflected that it was actually the later, modern designs of Baldwin House and the art library interior that, apart from Main, most appealed to him.[47] His employment of a medieval revival architectural style, however, gave Vassar some of its most beloved buildings. It also lent the appearance of traditional academic respectability to his most controversial program: euthenics.

Ellen Swallow Richards (Vassar 1870), the first woman admitted to the Massachusetts Institute of Technology, chemist and pioneer in the fields of sanitation and home economics, developed the term "euthenics" to describe a science that deals with the development of human well-being through the improvement of living conditions.[48] Through the study of euthenics, which combined child psychology, sanitation, nutrition, and design among other subjects, Richards claimed that life would improve both for individual families and for society as a whole.[49] Although Richards had died by the time of MacCracken's presidency, her follower, trustee Julia Lathrop (Vassar 1880), called for educational reform at the ceremonies marking MacCracken's inauguration and the college's fiftieth anniversary in October 1915.[50] Lathrop, a renowned leader in the field of social work, called for a center for scholarly research into family life and the professionalization of a woman's role in the household.[51] Although Taylor and other academics had resisted Richards's ideas as unscholarly, MacCracken heard them "like the sound of a trumpet."[52] He remarked, "The whole of higher education for women was still governed by the concepts developed when men were the only students and women went with the land."[53] In his mind, euthenics offered women an education that responded to their particular needs and interests.

Vassar's faculty, however, was less enthusiastic about the proposed new curriculum. In faculty meetings of 1922 and 1923, the administration presented the idea of a euthenics program.[54] Courses in nutrition, applied physiology, and child psychology would be added to fill out the program alongside existing courses. MacCracken envisioned euthenics as one of several program options within a broad and flexible curriculum. Since the Vassar faculty had only recently gained control over educational policy, MacCracken's interdisciplinary model was considered a threat to its new independence. Many were alarmed by the vocational aspect of the proposal, in particular its domestic science quality, which seemed to acknowledge and support traditional roles for women.

The deciding event occurred when Minnie Cumnock Blodgett (Vassar 1884) offered the college a building specifically for the new program. While the faculty controlled the curriculum, the trustees controlled decisions about building gifts. After much hesitation on both sides, the faculty narrowly accepted the curricular proposal in June 1924. The trustees

Mrs. Minnie Blodgett with President MacCracken at the dedication of Blodgett Hall, 1927

decided to accept Blodgett's gift of $500,000 for the construction of a euthenics building with an additional $50,000 promised to endow a mainte-nance fund.[55]

The new building was placed on Wing Farm, a property of 120 acres on the northeast side of the campus purchased by the college in 1923. It was in this part of the campus, separated from other classroom buildings, that the euthenics group, consisting of Wimpfheimer Nursery School (1927), Cushing Hall (1927), Blodgett Hall (1928), and Kenyon Gym (1933), was built.[56] MacCracken, who was closely concerned with all aspects of the col-lege's operation, was deeply involved in these construction projects and often expressed strong views about their styles, sites, and detailing. He strongly advocated the use of a medieval revival vocabulary for the architectural centerpiece of his presidency. The academic associations of the style tied his controversial program to more traditional scholarly pursuits.

Despite the support of MacCracken and many of the alumnae, the euthenics buildings, Blodgett in particular, were never completely used for their intended purpose. Possibly the most noteworthy part of the euthenics program was a summer institute held annually from 1926 to 1958 for alumnae and others who might benefit from courses such as child development or nutrition in their professional or family lives.[57] Within Vassar itself, however, the euthenics program floundered without broad faculty support as it came to be regarded by many as a gender-based limit to women's development. The domestic, traditional quality of the euthenics curriculum, which was underscored unconsciously by the cozy English manor house–style of its buildings, held little appeal for women trying to lead their students on to new frontiers.

The euthenics group's physical isolation from the rest of Vassar became a metaphor for its intellectual isolation, and in the years after World War II, the term disappeared altogether from the curriculum. Euthenics left its mark most clearly in the presence of Wimpfheimer and the college's enduring reputation in child development studies.

MacCracken himself is remembered today as a dynamic leader who successfully led the college into the modern age, although his interest in euthenics is largely forgotten. The obituary published in the *Vassar Quarterly* at the time of his death makes no mention of euthenics but records:

> It was during his presidency, and in large part due to him, that the image of Vassar as a truly liberal and progressive college actually took form. He was openly for women's suffrage from the start; he worked for civil rights and against racism, parochialism and intolerance in any form.... Within the college, these same guiding principles were in evidence... for he strove always to make it a more perfect microcosm of his democratic ideals. He believed in the students' ability to think for themselves, and in their right to be heard... he wanted to make every Vassar woman 'a citizen of the world.'[58]

The Blanding Years, 1946–64

When Sarah Gibson Blanding (1898–1985) stepped down from her presidency in the summer of 1964, trustees, faculty, students, and the general administration embraced her as their "mistress" of the great Vassar campus. They hailed her farewell with a poignant series of articles in the *Vassar*

*Sarah Gibson Blanding, Vassar's sixth president
(1946–64)*

Alumnae Magazine celebrating her vision, her commitment, and her many accomplishments, which included significant developments in Vassar's building infrastructure.[59] The flavor of these articles points to her enormous personal appeal as Vassar's first female president.

Sarah Gibson Blanding inaugurated her presidency in October of 1946, at a time of great cultural and political change following World War II and at the beginning of the cold war. In her inaugural address, Blanding spoke of the need to honor intellectual as well as spiritual themes in order to sustain a greater understanding of the human condition. She conducted her presidency with a delicate balance of these attributes as she guided her institution through the McCarthy years when higher education was a point of attack. *Vassar Alumnae Magazine* aptly described her character in the following way: "Her zest, her style, her humor, her dedication to excellence in all things," were, "as Matthew Vassar had demanded a hundred years ago, 'to things better than the best.'"[60]

During her presidency she administered an increase of 116 percent in the median faculty salaries, underscoring her conviction to retain and recruit the best faculty for Vassar. She supervised the development of a new curriculum, "emphasizing the value of independent work and offering unlimited opportunity for today's more mature and serious student to move ahead at her own pace."[61] Following her deep commitment to the development of women's education, Blanding encouraged her students to continue their studies in graduate school, and by 1963, over one third of them would do so, contrasting with the national trend. Blanding tripled Vassar's endowment and worked closely with the alumnae to ensure their support and loyalty to the college. In addition, she oversaw pioneering psychological research on "the characteristics of growth and change occurring during the college years."[62] Her intellectual leadership was reflected in a 1960 comparative chart in *Who's Who of American Women* that shows Vassar graduates with a significant lead over other similar institutions for both the numbers of entrants and the percentage of graduates listed.[63] In spite of her support for women's education, Blanding foresaw the diminishing viability of single-sex institutions of higher education. In *Full Steam Ahead in Poughkeepsie,* Blanding was cited as saying in 1966, "There is now real uncertainty about the future of women's colleges despite their splendid achievements, present high social esteem and the influence and loyalty of their alumnae."[64] However prescient this statement, coeducation would not take place until the next presidency.

Blanding, who had been the dean of the College of Home Economics at Cornell University, did not come to Vassar with a particular building agenda. One of her greatest legacies, however, would be her visionary spirit as a patron of architecture. She championed the building of Ferry House, Noyes House, Chicago Hall, and Watson Faculty Housing, as well as four major renovations to Main, Taylor, Thompson Library, and Davison House. She did not have a background in architecture but consulted with a very sophisticated group of advisors and donors on the selection of architects for her projects. Blanchette Hooker Rockefeller, head of the Trustee Building Committee (1951) and known for her work on the Museum of Modern Art board and her familiarity with avant-garde designers, was an important influence. In commissioning Marcel Breuer for Ferry House, Eero Saarinen for Noyes House, Paul Schweikher for Chicago Hall, and Carl Koch for the Watson Housing, Blanding selected not only the very best architects of the day, but also architects with an international vision and a modern sensibility.

In the context of the campus's diverse selection of architectural styles, Blanding encouraged the introduction of a new building vocabulary, a new cultural expression that would influence the evolving campus environment. She articulated Vassar's view of itself as a confident, assertive institution at the forefront of modern life. Carefully inserted into the existing campus fabric, Noyes and Chicago in particular, occupy sites that provide dramatic views of the modern designs. Noyes curves around the northeastern edge of the Circle creating a distinctive counterpoint to the soft forms of the defining flower and tree beds of the Circle. Chicago Hall, at the end of Josselyn's great lawn, was once silhouetted against the ornate collegiate

LEFT: *Chicago Hall*
RIGHT: *Noyes House, parlor*

Gothic design of the original Thompson Library. At night, its brightly lit interior emphasized the curving profile of its distinctive roof.

At Blanding's final trustee meeting of May 1964, the chairman of the board, John Wilkie, gave a small and moving speech in honor of her retirement, which concluded:

> All of us have had the occasion to express to her our admiration, our honor, our gratitude, our deep affection. She came to Vassar at a difficult time. She led with zest not only the College but 'the strenuous life.' She is civilized, in the wisest sense; she has been courageous; she has been compassionate. I suggest that we rise, as a very simple gesture of respect to a great lady.[65]

The Simpson Years, 1964–77

Despite Vassar's ongoing success as a women's college, Blanding had accurately predicted that the years of single-sex education were coming to an end, and that within a hundred years, no more than ten women's colleges would remain of the hundred or so in existence.[66] In fact, the Simpson years were marked by that very transformation from a premier Seven Sisters women's college to a fully coeducational institution. The story of this momentous decision is well documented in Elizabeth Daniels and Clyde Griffen's book, *Full Steam Ahead in Poughkeepsie.* In 1966 Alan Simpson met with Kingman Brewster, president of Yale, to discuss a possible affiliation with Yale University that would mean the relocation of Vassar to New Haven. Although Simpson seems to have favored this approach, there was opposition on many fronts, primarily faculty and alumnae. One significant argument against the move focused on the loss of Vassar's campus, the special environment that had shaped the school and its graduates. After almost two years of study, in 1968, Vassar made history with its announcement to go forward with coeducation. The trustees voted to accept men, to increase the enrollment, and to centralize the dining facilities, making way for the beginning of a new era. This institution would require a different infrastructure that included new kinds of residential, athletic, and social facilities, a transformation that Simpson was poised to undertake.

British-born Simpson left the University of Chicago where he had been the E. Donnelly Professor of History and dean of the college to become Vassar's president, beginning one year after President Kennedy's assassination. His period encompassed one of America's most challenging political and cultural times. At their twenty-fifth reunion, President Simpson wrote in the Class of 1972's yearbook: "We lived through historic and horrific times together. And survived! You gave me an exciting and

Presidents Blanding, Smith, and Simpson, c. 1980

sometimes rough time, but I learned a lot from you, and I hope you learned something from me. We were friends and I loved you."[67] This was a generous comment coming from a president whose term was marked by great change and upheaval in the college and in the country. From the American Civil Rights Movement to the war in Vietnam, to coeducation, Simpson moved from one crisis to another in his thirteen-year presidency. His greatest legacy lies not in his contributions to significant campus architecture or planning, but in his emphasis on curricular development, environmental initiatives, and in the planning for a new coeducational college—in short, building Vassar's future.

Vassar's social life had previously revolved around the life of each residential house and dining room. With the decision to centralize the dining facilities in the former Students' Building and the addition of a new student center in Main Building, the college began to offer a more centralized social experience that was balanced by the creation of a new set of residential options that included Terrace Apartments and Town Houses for groups of four to five students each. In order to meet the charge of an increased enrollment, Simpson was forced to build quickly and to abandon the many interesting proposals he had first initiated: a new dormitory by Hugh Stubbins, a new dining facility by I. M. Pei & Partners, a new experimental theater by John Johansen, and the study of a new dining hall/dorm by Polshek and Partners—all highly distinguished architects of the time. Instead, Simpson authorized the speedy construction of the Town Houses and immediately began the planning for the new College Center and Terrace

Apartments. In the first project of the Town Houses, Robert Hutchins, Vassar's consulting architect, assisted in the modification of a prefabricated housing system. Shortly thereafter, Shepley Bulfinch Richardson and Abbott built a well-planned new College Center as an addition and renovation to the back of Main. Designed by this old Bostonian firm founded by Henry Hobson Richardson, this plan transformed the ground floor space of Main Building. Jean Paul Carlhian, the firm's designer on this project, would then go on to work closely with Acorn Housing Inc. to complete the Terrace Apartments just one year later.

In addition to providing new residential and social infrastructure for the incoming coeducational students, Simpson began the transformation of the service buildings in the back of Main by converting the old power plant into a new experimental theater. Today this section of the campus has become a major hub of student activity. Through the vision of President Fergusson the rest of these buildings in Vassar's backyard have been fully renovated.

The only new academic building completed during Simpson's period was the Olmsted Hall of Biological Sciences by Sherwood, Mills and Smith, located on the southwest side of the science quad and completed in 1972.

The Smith Years, 1977–86

Virginia Smith, Vassar's eighth president, left her Washington post as the director of the Fund for Improvement of Postsecondary Education, an arm of the Department of Health, Education and Welfare, to lead the college in 1977. She came to Vassar with excellent credentials and experience in the study of education but little training in actual college or university life. In a tribute to Virginia Smith, the *Vassar Quarterly* noted:

> Historians of the college will find the accomplishments of the Smith years evidence of her analytical breadth: the improved fiscal status of the college, the additional buildings and restored grounds, the reorganized administrative structure, and the manuscript collection.[68]

In addition, she emphasized the importance of a liberal arts education, which needed to be protected against the emerging increase in undergraduate business programs, computer programs, and generally technical courses that were promoted at other institutions.

Smith's building program included some very interesting additions to the campus: the Seeley G. Mudd Chemistry Building by Perry Dean Rogers & Partners and the Walker Field House by Daniel F. Tully & Associates, both of which demonstrate innovative use of new materials and technologies. With the Walker Field House, Smith continued the development of the east campus, which would provide the kind of athletic infrastructure necessary for a coeducational student body. Strategically located near the golf course, this field house visually completed the linear profile of the Terrace Apartments as they marched up the hill toward the east. Both the Terrace Apartments and the Walker Field House were thoughtfully designed with respect to their adjacent landscape, using a visual vocabulary of peaked roofs to complement the distant views and surrounding landscape. The Seeley G. Mudd Building, home of the chemistry department and located on the north side of the science quad, where the Vassar Brothers Laboratory once stood, finally completed this quadrangle.

Smith's nine-year presidency marked one of the shortest in Vassar's history. During this time, she completed two buildings but was not able to successfully tackle the restoration of the campus grounds, which were beginning to show signs of wear and tear after years of neglect. This task remained for Smith's successor, Frances Daly Fergusson. Smith did designate 276 acres of the Vassar Farm as an ecological preserve, however, laying the foundation for the development of the environmental sciences program and the new Priscilla Bullitt Collins Field Station, which was built in the 1990s.

The Fergusson Years, 1986–

Frances Daly Fergusson, Vassar's ninth president, came to the college from Bucknell University in 1986, where she had been the provost and vice president for academic affairs. Looking back, she said that she had two immediate, yet far-reaching, goals when she first arrived at Vassar: "to reverse the corrosive decline of the physical plant" and "to instill at Vassar a renewed spirit of community, friendliness, pride and happiness."[69] At the time of her inauguration, the dominant impression of the campus was one of faded glory in the midst of asphalt sprawl. The splendid old buildings needed renewal and renovation to meet the demands of a contemporary culture. The community, too, was frayed around the edges:

> My immediate perception was of an institution afraid to proclaim itself an excellent place, an institution that was frankly worried that the Vassar of today might not be the equal of the Vassar of yesterday. And yet, by all objective measures, we were very good: we had a faculty and student body of the highest quality. We were also, however, an institution with some fractures in our social structure, not enough respectful dialogue, and failures in simple kindness and friendly engagement.[70]

Her two goals—the physical plant and the morale of the community—were linked in Fergusson's mind. An architectural historian who took

Frances Daly Fergusson, Vassar's president since 1986

her degrees from Wellesley and Harvard, she was highly aware of the way physical spaces affect the quality of human transactions and behavior. She set about the reclamation of the campus, and at the same time, she engaged the community—faculty, staff, student leaders, and alumnae/i—in discussions about the campus and facilities, and in the planning of renovations and new construction.

During her tenure, she initiated and brought to completion what was then the largest fundraising campaign ever undertaken by a liberal arts college and raised over $200 million. Supported by the fruits of that campaign, Vassar has addressed deferred maintenance needs; renovated the landscape; steadily improved the living, learning, and teaching environments for students and faculty; and added new buildings and spaces that directly support the intellectual and recreational interests of the community.

The well-orchestrated planning process began in 1988 when Vassar hired Sasaki Associates to develop a new master plan for the campus. The firm undertook a major historical study of the campus plan with an aim to improve the vehicular circulation and the pedestrian experience, and to refurbish the landscape design in keeping with Matthew Vassar's dream. Fergusson has successfully acted on the suggestions of this master plan. Much of the unnecessary paving has been removed, and new plantings as well as stone curb details and new outdoor lighting have animated the central campus. The arboretum has begun a major renovation, with the new addition of the Priscilla Bullitt Collins '42 Trail, near the Fonteyn Kill.

The next phase of the planning process comprised three parts: the classroom, residential, and student life master plans. The classroom master plan subcommittee, led by Ellenzweig Associates, for instance, did an exhaustive inventory of all classrooms and explored ways to implement improvements accordingly. This thorough analysis provided the basis for a ten-year plan to develop and renovate all of the classrooms and laboratories to meet today's technological and pedagogical needs, and a companion plan to renovate all residential space to accommodate contemporary lifestyles.

Implementing these various plans has entailed the recycling of some buildings for new purposes, the thorough renovation of others, and new construction of a number of buildings. The primary site for building recycling was the former building and grounds complex behind Main Building (see pp. 117–121). Simpson had already begun the "recycling program" with the conversion of the powerhouse into a black-box theater, the Powerhouse Theater. Under Fergusson's leadership, the transformation of the service area continued in accordance with the Sasaki plan, including the redesign of the old coal bin to become the Susan Stein Shiva Theater and the development of a terraced walkway, known as the Fisher Passage. The Old Laundry Building is now home to the Development Office and the Computer Science Department; and trade shops became the Computer Center, the Doubleday Studio Art Building, and the ALANA Center.

In accordance with the classroom, residential, and student life plans, several renovations of existing facilities have been completed (Blodgett Hall, Thompson Library, Ferry House, the interior of Noyes, Jewett House, and the Students' Building). Still others are on the schedule (Kenyon Hall and the Art Library in Van Ingen are next).

The major buildings completed during Fergusson's presidency include the Frances Lehman Loeb Art Center and the Center for Drama and Film (formerly Avery Hall) by Cesar Pelli & Associates, the Class of 1951 Observatory by Roth and Moore Architects, the Athletics and Fitness Center by Cannon Associates, the Martha Rivers and E. Bronson Ingram Library addition by Hardy Holzman Pfeiffer Associates, the Priscilla Bullitt Collins Field Station, and the new Terrace Apartments.

In 1997 Fergusson quipped, "It is my firm intention to go down in Vassar history as the president who has removed the most asphalt from Vassar."[71] She certainly has secured that position for herself. But she will also be remembered as the president who moved Vassar confidently into the new millennium, transforming the gracious but frayed campus into a visually striking, vibrant center of intellectual and social activity.

Priscilla Bullitt Collins '42 Trail

From Racetrack to Academic Park: The Legacy of the Landscape

Winston Churchill once said, "We shape our buildings and afterwards our buildings change us."[1] This is true not only of our buildings but of our landscapes as well, and nowhere is this more apparent than at Vassar.

The experience of arriving at Vassar, through the arched opening of Taylor Hall, is a glorious transition into one of America's great academic parks. The grand impression made by Main Building sets the tone as one approaches this formidable original construction on axis with the entrance. This is the inaugural experience to a campus that includes a rich collection of buildings set into a landscape plan known for its picturesque and intimate qualities. This constructed campus was once a flat and barren field. The story of its development reveals how its physical transformation relates to its pedagogy, and how both affected the character of the place and its graduates.

The evolution of the campus, its site planning, landscape design, and architectural character, were not generated from a single grand vision, as was the case in Jefferson's Academic Village, for example. Vassar's development followed an evolutionary process that involved the participation of the founder Matthew Vassar, the administration, the students, the faculty, and the alumnae/i. In 1914 President Taylor wrote:

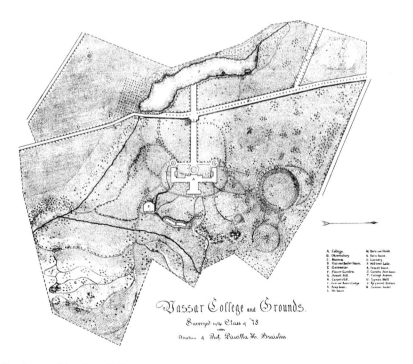

Rendering of site plan, 1878

No institution should enter upon building without a thorough study of the possibilities for fifty years. Built without such a plan, the Vassar campus is a fortunate result on the whole, gained by the steady hold of a few men and women who worked many years together, on a half recognized vision and with a whole-hearted and unselfish purpose.[2]

Matthew Vassar, in consultation with Milo Jewett, chose the site of the old Mill Cove Estate for the college's campus, 198 acres large and situated 3 miles east of the Hudson River. They agreed that a female college should be located away from the traffic of the city and the Hudson River in a more secluded and protected setting. Vassar wrote:

> More desirable than anything else for the health and comfort of the inmates of the projected college, was the large pond known as Mill Cove Pond of pure spring water and whose outlet had for years turned a mill wheel, presented an assurance that all bountiful supply would be given.[3]

In addition to its secluded nature and its available natural resources, the site also provided Vassar with an opportunity to construct a monumental building as a signifier of his own charitable contribution to society. A more spectacular site along the Hudson, which he had initially sought, would not have been suitable for such a building. The Mill Cove Estate, formerly the Dutchess County Racetrack, was a perfect tabula rasa for the new college.

The positioning of the campus's first structure, Main, was controversial. Vassar had wanted to align it with Raymond Avenue but President Jewett convinced him that placement along the cardinal points would serve as an "educating force," and so Main was oriented directly west, toward, but not in view of the great Hudson River. This early decision to place the college within its larger geographical context was to remain an important force in the future development of this section of the campus, associating the college with its larger habitat—the Hudson River Valley. All of the buildings located on the flat plain near Main follow this initial alignment. Later, as the college expanded, buildings along the Casperkill and Fonteyn Kill would be located in relation to the local landscape, rather than on the established axis, and their siting would follow the topography of the creek beds. These two contiguous systems are today seamlessly joined by the landscape plan that has evolved incrementally and has been largely created by the Vassar community itself.

Main Building, which housed most of the college functions in the early years, dominated the bare and open plain. Its architect, James Renwick, Jr., held the contract for the site and landscape planning as well as for the building design. Vassar himself, however, took over the supervision of the grounds, initiating his own landscape program.

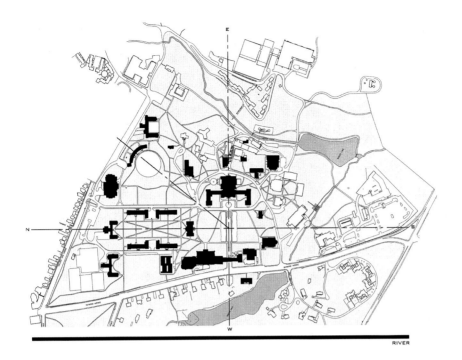

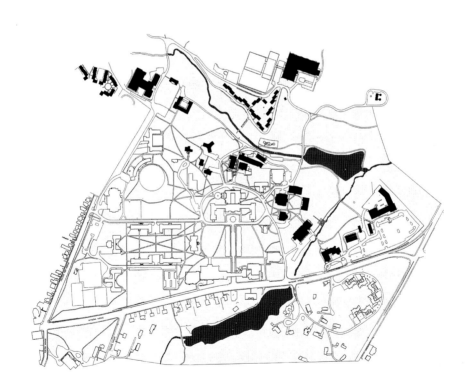

TOP: *Diagram of buildings located along the cardinal axis*
BOTTOM: *Campus buildings that follow the natural topography of the creek beds*

Vassar's earlier association with Andrew Jackson Downing formed the basis of his approach. Both men were Hudson River Valley natives, and Downing had designed the house and gardens for Vassar's Hudson River estate, Springside, located only a few miles from the college. Downing, a horticulturist by training, is considered to be America's first landscape architect. His *Treatise on the Theory and Practice of Landscape Gardening* had tremendous influence on the development of this art form in America and was well known to Vassar. Downing believed that gardens should be both "beautiful" and "picturesque":

> The Beautiful is nature or art obeying the universal laws of perfect existence (i.e. Beauty), easily, freely, harmoniously, and without the *display* of power. . . . The Picturesque is nature or art obeying the same laws rudely, violently, irregularly, and often displaying power only.[4]

Downing's premature death in 1852 prevented his direct involvement in the design of the campus, but his influence resonates throughout Vassar's early planning schemes. At the time of the college's opening in 1865, Vassar had overseen the planting of one thousand new trees on this barren landscape. In the next three years, he would continue to direct the planning of his great experiment. He doubled the size of the Mill Cove Lake (Vassar Lake) and set aside seventy acres for the purpose of ornamental planting. These early plantings form the basis of the landscape plan we see today, following the logic of a picturesque vocabulary and referential to the Hudson River Valley.

Vassar's sudden death on June 23, 1868, as he was reading his annual address to the board of trustees, shocked the college community. In emotional haste, President Raymond and the board reconvened to propose the erection of a statue of the founder. They resolved, "to employ one of the best landscapists in the community to prepare a complete plan for laying out and ornamenting the College grounds with special reference to securing the best location for a Statue of the Founder."[5] In response to this objective, Frederick Law Olmsted and Calvert Vaux, well known for their 1858 Central Park competition plan, visited the campus in August 1868, and made "an outline sketch of roads, paths & other improvements, which was submitted."[6] However, no drawings were ever found, and there is no evidence that any substantive planning resulted from this visit. Throughout the college's history, the administration has engaged professional planners and landscape architects but has rarely followed their advice. Instead they formulated their own plans in consultation with the board, the faculty, students, and alumnae/i.

Following Vassar's death, the administration, faced with financial uncertainty, focused its attention on the economic stability of the college

Rendering of Tree Day ceremonies, the burial of class relics, 1888

rather than its physical development. Hence, it was the early college women, discouraged by their barren environment, who began their own landscape program. In 1867 the first class planted ivy on Main Building, followed by the planting of a great swamp oak and a weeping elm near Main's front door. Ever since, each class has contributed or adopted a class tree, initiating one of Vassar's most important early traditions—the Tree Ceremony.

Photos of Tree Day demonstrate not only its importance to the development of the landscape but also its significance in creating a profound connection between the land and the college community. The

Tree Day ceremony, early twentieth century

grounds superintendent, the faculty, and the administration all helped in the designation of tree locations, planting different sections of the campus at different times. The tree ceremonies became a cultlike event held in secret with elaborate costumes and dances designed to worship the tree. The ritual culminated in the burial of the class records and relics next to or under the tree, a tradition that tied the women to this land and that fostered alumnae support for its development. The arboretum endowment, given by the class of 1875 at their fiftieth reunion in 1925, is one of the most influential examples of these contributions.

Other stories convey a similar pattern. The Circle was Vassar's first real garden, located just west of the observatory. Originally laid out in the 1860s as an exercise area, it was soon appropriated by Dr. Alida Avery, professor of physiology and hygiene. She organized the Floral Society, in which students cared for the garden themselves, turning exercise into a useful and aesthetic mission. Flowers became so important to the quality of life at the college that Vassar built a greenhouse in 1886 solely for their growth and distribution to all of the college's public rooms.

These early landscape transformations orchestrated by the faculty and students parallel an equally interesting pedagogical development, that of the study of ecology at Vassar. A German disciple of Darwin, Ernst Haeckel, first used the word "Oecologie" in 1866, to classify the study of living organisms in relation to their environment. One of Vassar's most distinguished alumnae, Ellen Swallow Richards (Vassar 1870), promoted this new area of study. As the first woman graduate of the Massachusetts Institute of Technology, Richards developed new methods for testing purity in food and drinking water. She was the founder of the American Home Economics Movement and is now considered one of America's pioneers in the field of ecology. As a trustee of Vassar College in 1894, Richards demonstrated her commitment to her profession and her alma mater. The college had been dumping its sewage into the Casperkill. In response to a proposal by the area residents, the college was poised to accept a plan to pipe its sewage all the way to the Hudson River. Richards reacted to this by saying, "It seems to me that an educational institution should lead rather than follow."[7]

When asked how she would remedy the problem, she proceeded to design a new sewage disposal plant, thus saving the river from pollution and saving the college the cost of a six-mile pipeline. Her interests were reinforced by many others such as Helen Clark Putnam, who taught physical education in the 1870s and later gave Vassar a conservation fund of nearly half a million dollars specifically to initiate an academic program on ecology and conservation. Over the following century, Vassar would become a leading educational institution in the field of environmental studies.

President Taylor oversaw the period of Vassar's greatest physical expansion by adding more than twenty new structures during his twenty-seven-year presidency. Taylor and his board struggled with the placement of these new buildings, which included the quad residences, the chapel, the library, and the Students' Building, among others. The siting of these new structures followed the geometric logic of Main's orientation, set on the cardinal points. During this expansive period, the college again hired Frederick Olmsted to assist in the configuration of the north campus. Olmsted suggested that the new residential buildings be configured in what he called an "echelon plan," which would have placed the dorms in two diagonal lines opening to the north. The board, along with its consulting architects, dismissed this proposal in favor of their own preferred quad arrangement, which we see today. When the chapel and library were completed, the board passed a resolution to preserve the openness of the lawn between Main, Rockefeller, the library, and the chapel. They reasoned correctly that Main needed a large open space to be properly viewed and appreciated.

As the building infrastructure emerged, so did a series of exterior spaces such as Main's lawn and the quad. Articulated as regular geometric spaces in plan, their formality is not reinforced by their subsequent landscape designs. The quad has its main building entries on the exterior of the quadrangle space, which tends to weaken the importance of its interior space. The tree-lined diagonal paths emphasize movement through the quad rather than reinforcing the enclosure as a place to be. This is also true of the lawn in front of Main. It is bifurcated by the entry road with its adjacent rows of trees. Each side has beautiful places to be discovered but there is no great space here that defines a campus center. These examples are indicative of one of the primary qualities of Vassar—that this landscape favors the individual experience over the collective. Vassar has no Jeffersonian "lawn"—no primary exterior space from which one may feel the character of the college. Here the spirit of the place unfolds slowly, through a complex series of highly articulated landscapes that interact with their inhabitants and promote the development of the individual spirit. In 1920 *The Women's Home Companion* published a comparative study of the Seven Sisters colleges, writing, "Smith turns out the doer, Wellesley, the student, Vassar, the adventurer, Bryn Mawr, the social philosopher, Mt. Holyoke the conservative. . . . From Vassar come the young adventurers, the pioneers in curious fields, the radicals."[8] Naturally, many aspects of college life shaped these graduates, but Vassar's physical environment, both its eclectic architecture and its interactive landscape, were contributing influences in this characterization.

In spite of Taylor's successful leadership in orchestrating the early master plan, he yearned for a comprehensive plan for Vassar's future development. In 1905 he hired Samuel Parsons, a prominent landscape architect, to develop a new master plan for the college. The Parsons firm designed a fifteen-acre campus plan for the area south of Vassar Lake. This beaux-arts configuration had Raymond Avenue running straight through the complex. To the east, behind the chapel, Parsons added ten acres of a "naturalistic" garden. Although the board voted to accept the proposal, it was never executed. The plan, however, is an interesting artifact as it naively reflects the duality of the formal and informal site developments already present on the campus.

When President MacCracken began his term in 1915, the campus had grown to over six hundred acres, half of which were devoted to the Vassar Farm. There were forty buildings on the campus, and the landscape had begun to mature. In MacCracken's thirty-one-year tenure he would oversee the development of that emerging campus plan and make several additions to it. MacCracken wrote of his land acquisitions:

> Now we added the Pheil farm of a hundred and ten acres, which we named for our beloved farmer Albert Flager. The Worrell farm of fifty-four, the Wing farm of one hundred and twenty acres, were added in 1924. The Hughes farm of fifteen was secured to provide for possible storage and unloading facilities by the railroad track to the north.[9]

The buildings added under his presidency generally follow the planning principles that owe allegiance to the local topography. They are situated

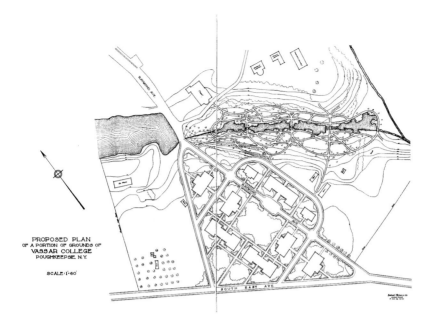

Proposed campus plan by Samuel Parsons, 1905

to reflect the special quality of their immediate surroundings, near the existing creek beds. These areas are characteristic of the most picturesque part of the campus, where the arboretum was developed.

In 1925, with the receipt of the arboretum endowment from the class of 1875, MacCracken began its planning, consulting with the superintendent of grounds, Henry E. Downer, a well-known botanist from England. Describing the arboretum, MacCracken wrote:

> It will be seen that, as outlined, a continuous belt of planting from the Vassar Lake to beyond the Euthenics group would be established, on land hardly likely to be taken for building sites. The development of what is now mostly rough along these lines would have great educational value in the study of plant material as well as produce good landscape effects.[10]

After having established this initial plan, the college conferred with the Olmsted Brothers firm, which had already been retained at Vassar to design the landscape for Skinner Hall and Alumnae House, and instructed them to complete the drawings.

Today the arboretum is one of Vassar's most important landscape features. Its layout has given visual structure to the creek beds and lakes, integrating them into the larger campus design, and thereby mediating the

Graduation at the Outdoor Amphitheater, 1952

two orientation systems of the buildings on campus. The arboretum now covers the entire main grounds with over two hundred species of native and introduced trees. Equally important, it is a pedagogical tool—trees have names and identities, and in the tradition of Thoreau, these trees have become "neighbors" to those who live in this community. The landscape is understood to be dynamic and an integral part of the educational experience.

MacCracken also oversaw the addition of several special landscape features, including Sunset Lake, the outdoor amphitheater, the Shakespeare Garden, the Dutchess County Ecological Laboratory, the golf course, and the outdoor classroom. In each case the Vassar community itself designed and/or built these spaces, demonstrating once again the traditional collaborative synthesis of the college's physical and intellectual goals.

Thoughtfully designed by resident landscape architect Loring Underwood, the amphitheater has hosted many theatrical performances as well as the annual graduation ceremony. The graduates face east toward the podium with Sunset Lake in the distance. As they move forward to receive their diplomas, they must cross the bridge over the constructed gully in this final rite of passage. Their graduation is memorialized in the landscape.

In 1916 the Shakespeare Garden was built through the collaborative efforts of the English and botany departments. The garden was planned and planted by the students and faculty themselves, using seeds they obtained from Stratford-upon-Avon. The garden is a formal space set into the side of the hill with a romantic view of Skinner Hall in the background, providing an outdoor destination for contemplation and intimate gatherings, including weddings.

In contrast to the formality of this space, another type of garden emerged on campus during this period. Dr. Edith Roberts, professor of botany and author of *The Role of Plant Life in the History of Dutchess County*, created the Dutchess County Outdoor Ecological Laboratory in 1922—the first of its kind in the nation. It was a landscaped area in which trees, shrubs, herbs, fungi, and ferns were planted in groupings to imitate their natural habitat and growth patterns. The modern-day version of this garden is the Priscilla Bullitt Collins '42 Trail (1995) located just south of the Shakespeare Garden adjacent to the Fonteyn Kill. These different kinds of gardens at Vasssar exemplify the richness of this constructed environment that shows both a formal manipulation of the landscape as well as respect for and reinforcement of the existing terrain.

With the purchase of Wing Farm, the college had expanded its holdings eastward. On the far side of the Casperkill, the golf course opened in 1930, setting the precedent to develop this side of the campus with more athletic facilities. The students and faculty laid out the course themselves,

Students building the Shakespeare Garden, 1916

building it with borrowed money from the college. Its spectacular location afforded views to the Hudson River Valley.

Besides the Olmsted Brothers firm, MacCracken had also employed another high-profile landscape architect, Beatrix Farrand, designer of Dumbarton Oaks in Washington, D.C., and the Rockefeller gardens in Seal Harbor, Maine, to work on specific areas of the campus. It is difficult to know the full extent of her involvement as few records remain. One exception is that of a plan of the entrance to Main and areas surrounding Kendrick House. The Main drawing indicates exterior boundaries of evergreens with a series of flowering plants in basically symmetrical groupings near the entry drive. Kendrick was to be planted with other flowering plants such as azaleas.[11] MacCracken never mentions Farrand in his book, *The Hickory Limb,* so it is difficult to know if any real changes occurred in the landscape plan as a result of these proposals.

MacCracken's interest in Vassar's landscape development extended beyond the physical realm and included a related educational mission. With the Helen Gates Putnam Endowment for Conservation, he began to plan for a new graduate division in conservation, drawing on an interdisciplinary group of faculty and departments. Upon acceptance of this gift he wrote:

> The conservation of the American landscape . . . is thus seen to be important not only for its economic results, but also for its results in human well being. We hope to obtain knowledge, which will enable us to build soundly for the future in directing the attention of the student body of Vassar to their responsibility as American citizens for making their country a land of which they may be able to say with truth. It is good for us to be here.[12]

With the commencement of World War II, however, these new conservation courses could not be realized until a decade later.

By the beginning of Blanding's presidency in 1946, Vassar's basic infrastructure and landscape had been well established, and although new buildings would later be added to the campus, the landscape plan did not change dramatically. The campus's rich, picturesque quality provided continuity for the diverse collection of buildings and styles found here. Blanding's building additions, which may be considered the most avant-garde of any period, found a comfortable home in this campus plan. The landscape became the negotiating element between the new architectural language of these international-style buildings and those of earlier, more traditional periods on campus.

Simpson began his presidency in 1964 with plans for several new building projects, which were ultimately abandoned in favor of expedient and appropriate solutions to accommodate the new coeducational student

Aerial view of college, 1959

body and the increase in enrollment. In lieu of nurturing the college land-scape, he focused his attention on the larger environmental issues that had begun to emerge nationally and regionally. He and his faculty initiated a new course entitled "The River," which brought together an interdisciplinary faculty group to study the Hudson River and its environment. Of this initiative he wrote:

> Any study of man's relation to his environment involves so many diffi-cult questions about our use of resources, natural and otherwise, that no one field of knowledge is competent to deal adequately with them. So 'The River' is, of necessity, an interdisciplinary course. This semester fourteen members of the faculty from the social and natural sciences and from art are relating their specialized knowledge to a common problem: the protection and development of the resources of the Hudson Valley for the increased well being of its inhabitants.[13]

The River Project became critical to the long-term mission, initi-ated by Governor Rockefeller, to save and preserve the Hudson River, and today we see the results of those early efforts. In 1976 President Smith con-tinued to emphasize this theme by committing 276 acres, the southern half of the college farm, as an ecological preserve. President Fergusson in turn added the Priscilla Bullitt Collins Field Station to house the growing curriculum in environmental science.

When she assumed the presidency in 1986, Fergusson immediately focused her attention on the preservation of the ailing landscape that had deteriorated over the past twenty-five years. In 1988 Fergusson hired the landscape and planning firm of Sasaki Associates to develop a comprehensive master plan for the maintenance and preservation of the historical structure of the landscape with an emphasis on the pedestrian experience. The firm outlined a well-conceived plan to properly rebuild many of the primary roads, curbs, walks, and adjacent lawns including a new outdoor lighting system. This plan also included the renewal of the arboretum with suggestions to reintegrate Vassar Lake into the life of the college. The recommendation of the report to remove many of the non-academic facilities from the center of campus subsequently led President Fergusson to develop and renovate the industrial buildings at the back of Main as a new college center, where the strategic addition of the Fisher Passage effectively connects the east campus to the original main grounds.

Of the many new buildings added to the campus during Fergusson's presidency, the Class of 1951 Observatory has special significance in the way it relates to the campus landscape plan and its history. The original observatory (1864) was the college's eye to the great universe beyond. Secluded from the outside world, early Vassar women found an outlet from their confined environment in this special space. The placement of the new observatory on the highest elevation of the main campus has not only been a practical consideration but a symbolic one as well. From this locale one can look west over Vassar's main campus in the foreground to the great Hudson River Valley in the distance. The two worlds have finally come together in the presence of the greater universe, completing the landscape cycle.

The story of Vassar's landscape is also the story of this famous college. From its bare beginnings as a racetrack to its rich and picturesque quality of today, Vassar has developed a unique environment, which juxtaposes both formal and informal spaces, and secluded and open landscapes, all of which are seamlessly connected in a coherent and eloquent whole. The resultant campus is one of America's most beautiful. Its fabrication from within has reinforced and promoted the development of one of the nation's earliest academic traditions in the study of ecology, land conservation, and a deep appreciation of the American landscape. Vassar's own community created this environment, and in turn that environment has shaped their characters, their identities, and their values.

MacCracken recounted in his book, *The Hickory Limb*, a conversation he had with a student's mother, who said: "All I needed was just to walk around Vassar grounds, in order to make my choice. Any college that is so kind to its trees is sure to be kind to my daughter."[14]

TOP: *Priscilla Bullitt Collins '42 Trail*
MIDDLE: *Campus walkway*
BOTTOM: *View from Ely Hall*

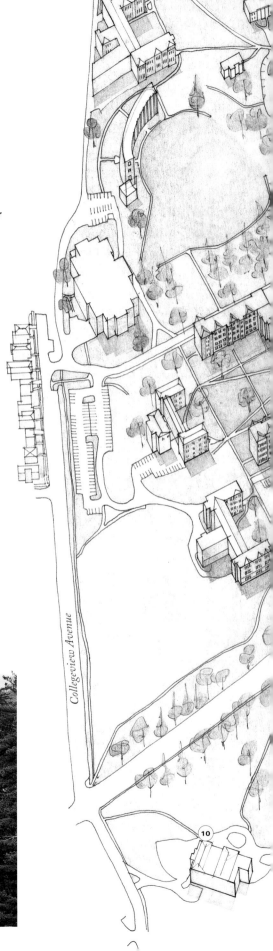

Raymond Avenue

Vassar Lake

Main Building, front facade

1. Main Building

James Renwick, Jr., 1865;

dining room and kitchen extension, James S. Post, 1872;

ground floor remodeling, Cesar Pelli, 1996

Thompson Annex

Francis R. Allen, 1893;

kitchen and dining room reconstruction, Allen & Collens, 1918;

ground floor remodeling, John McAndrew, 1937;

remodeling and removal of Thompson Annex, Goldstone & Dearborn, 1959

College Center addition

Jean Paul Carlhian, Shepley Bulfinch Richardson and Abbott, 1974–75

College Center additions and renovations, Sloan Architects, PC, 2001

Renwick's Second Empire masterpiece, Main, has dominated the Vassar campus since its completion in 1865.[1] As the center of Vassar life, the building has undergone many renovations and additions throughout the college's history. Combining residential, academic, and administrative functions under one roof, Main continues to encompass many aspects of collegiate life. Designed originally to house all college facilities apart from those necessary for the study of astronomy and physical education, the building is massive and was in fact claimed to be the largest building in the U.S. at the time of its construction.

The idea of Main as one structure with lengthy corridors was developed by Thomas Tefft, a well-known school architect who first received the commission for the new college.[2] Tefft's drawing of 1856 shows a series of fifty-foot-long two-story passageways connecting five separate three-story blocks. The building would have been broken into separate units, visibly articulated by the distinct blocks, while the sense of a unified community was expressed through the connecting corridors. Tefft's design was in the popular Lombard Romanesque style for which he was well known. In preparation for his final scheme for Vassar, he went abroad on a study tour of Lombardy and northern Italy. Due to his untimely death in 1859 while in Florence, his plan for Vassar was never executed.

The commission for Main was passed on to his better-known contemporary, James Renwick, Jr. (1818–95),[3] whose plans for Main were approved by the board and Matthew Vassar by spring of 1861. Renwick, also best known for his use of medieval revival styles, was a prestigious choice for the pioneering institution. His design of Grace Church in New York City (1843–46) won him national recognition and was followed by his prize-winning entry in the 1846 competition for the Smithsonian Institution in Washington, D.C. During the 1850s, Renwick began to employ the Second Empire style, first for the Cruger Mansion in New York City (1853–54) and then for public institutions such as the Small Pox Hospital of 1853–56(?) on Blackwell's Island in New York, which, like Vassar's Main Building, was modeled on the Tuileries. Matthew Vassar had admired the sixteenth-century French palace on a trip to Europe. The Elias P. Magoon Collection of Art, given by Vassar to the college in 1864, includes a print of the Tuileries with several inscriptions in his hand which note the similarities between the two buildings.[4] In fact, his portrait of 1861 by Charles Loring Elliott shows Vassar in a pose very similar to that found in Franz Xaver Winterhalter's portrait of Napoleon III of 1852–59, then resident in the Tuileries. In Vassar's portrait, Main Building parallels the position of the Tuileries in the Winterhalter composition.[5]

Renwick's version of the palace was, however, considerably simpler than contemporary Renwick Second Empire structures such as the Corcoran Gallery in Washington, D.C. (1859–71). At Vassar, Renwick preserved the grand scale of his French model while using more modest materials. Main is built of brick with a slate mansard roof. For ornament, Renwick relied on pairs of engaged brick pilasters to emphasize the corners of Main's projecting pavilions and stair towers. Brick string courses and cornices articulate the building's horizontal divisions. The most elaborate—those found between the fourth and fifth stories of the central and terminal pavilions—employ a simple dentil pattern. Bluestone was used for the keystones of the many arched windows and selected elements of the building's trim. A more polychromatic quality dominated Main's original appearance as the bricks were set in black mortar with a roof of purple and green slates. Rosalie McKenna's study of Main notes that Renwick's use of color at Vassar followed Calvert

Vaux's theory of the importance of complementary colors.[6] Vaux had followed these principles in his design of Springside, Matthew Vassar's house,
in 1851. White was to be avoided as buildings placed in a "natural" setting
should not stand out in stark contrast to their environment but blend in with
the landscape. The alternating diagonal stripes of green and purple slate on
the dome roof were intended to carry the eye upward and outward.

While Renwick followed Tefft's concept of lengthy corridors, he
rejected the earlier idea of a series of visibly separate units connected by
passageways. Instead, Renwick's design created a more integrated, unified
building that still expressed the hierarchy of the college community through
the articulation of its facade. The massive five-hundred-foot width of the
structure is broken into three parts with a central projecting five-story pavilion flanked by a pair of four-story blocks. The central block housed the chief
officers of the college—President Raymond and Lady Principal Hannah
Lyman. The front of the second, third, and fourth floors was partly occupied
by Raymond's offices and apartment. Lyman's residence was opposite
Raymond's quarters on the third floor. The pavilions at the end of each of
the 164–foot-long wings housed the faculty of professorial rank and their
families in scaled-down versions of the central facade. Students and the
twenty college teachers—instructors who were not qualified to hold the
rank of professor—lived along the building's lengthy corridors. Students
lived in suites of three bedrooms and a parlor along these unusually wide
(twelve feet) and well-lit corridors, which ran along the front of the building
and added a layer of privacy to the residential quarters. They also provided
space for exercise in bad weather, reflecting Matthew Vassar's belief that
fresh air and exercise were critical to the well-being of young women.
Before the completion of the Calisthenium in 1866, physical education

Main Building, seen from Taylor Gate

Main Building, corridor

classes were held here. The unfortunate side effect of this arrangement was that one bedroom of each suite had no natural light or ventilation with its only window opening onto the corridor.

Another wing projecting to the rear of Main originally housed the chapel and dining room. In this less visible part of the building were rooms for most of the college servants. Essentially, the whole college community (faculty, students, and servants) originally lived and worked in Main. The most notable exception was Maria Mitchell, professor of astronomy, who lived with her father in the college observatory.

The hierarchy evident in the facade also had a horizontal expression. As an engraving of 1864 shows (see *Introduction*, p. 6), Main's original entrance was on the second floor, into a vestibule flanked by the college parlors and president's apartments. Classrooms and the library were also found in the central section of the building. The art collection was housed on the top floor under the domical roof, whose windows admitted natural light into the gallery below. The second floor of the central part of Main remains the home of its parlors, still elegantly decorated in a Victorian style and the site of frequent student gatherings, including daily tea. The presidential and other administrative offices are also found here. The third floor housed the offices and rooms of the lady principal, while the ground or first floor functioned as a kind of basement. Its low ceilings and utilitarian features reveal its original role as the primary work space of the college, inhabited by servants and holding service rooms such as the kitchen, laundry, linen room, and pantry along with a few classrooms.

Main Building was designated a National Historic Landmark in 1986 in acknowledgment of its architectural significance and its importance as a landmark in the history of women's education. It has been listed in the National Register of Historic Places since 1973, yet its design has not always been so revered. In 1893, to relieve overcrowding in the library, an unsightly wing was added that projected forward from the central facade (see p. 12). Known as Uncle Fred's Nose, in honor of its donor, Frederick Ferris Thompson, the addition was long regarded as an eyesore. In 1959, under President Blanding, Uncle Fred's Nose was razed to the cheers of student onlookers. The facade was returned to its original design by the architectural firm of Goldstone and Dearborn with the omission of the stairs leading to the second story. At this point, the ground floor housed the building's heavily used principal entrance. A 1937 remodeling had created a series of student rooms on the ground floor and space for the Vassar Cooperative Bookstore. The snack bar, post office, and several administrative offices were also housed on what had become the main street of the college. After extensive study, Goldstone and Dearborn judged it impractical to recreate a second-story exterior entrance. Instead, a massive porch, using Renwick details, was added to "provide a visual weight equivalent to the original staircase and yet honestly express the important new functions of the former 'basement.'"[7] In 1996 architect Cesar Pelli created a brighter and more welcoming entrance to the college's Main Building with his colorful reworking of the ground floor and his placement of the entrance to the College Center on axis with the entrance at the rear of Main.

Coeducation brought with it the need for new and renovated physical space. Apart from providing living quarters for the new students, it was also necessary to create more social spaces. Certainly, one of the most dramatic changes to campus life came with the 1974 renovation of and addition to Main's rear wing—resulting in the new College Center. The creation of this new hub restored Main to its original symbolic function—as the center of campus life.

The selected architectural firm, Shepley Bulfinch Richardson and Abbott, is an old Bostonian firm founded in 1874 by New Orleans–born

Main Building, Rose Parlor

Main Building

Henry Hobson Richardson, who remains one of America's most distinguished nineteenth-century architects. He is known for such buildings as
Trinity Church, Boston; Allegheny County Courthouse and Jail in Pittsburgh;
and the Marshall Field Wholesale Store in Chicago. Throughout the firm's
long and successful history, it established a strong reputation in the area of
institutional work, particularly science buildings.

Designed by Jean Paul Carlhian, this new addition represents a
clear commitment to architectural preservation and renovation. It wraps
around the east wing of Main in a U-shaped configuration, preserving the
original Second Empire Renwick facades by incorporating them into the
adjacent spaces. The resultant bifurcation of the space brought about two
courtyards rather than one central space. These two symmetrical double-
height skylit courtyards are located on either side of the old Main volume
and include dining facilities, a post office, an exhibition space, and a more
recently renovated bookstore at the lower level. The upper level contains
bridges to the old two-story-high dining room, now the Villard Room, and
is used for special functions. In 1918, following a fire that destroyed this
room, Allen & Collens renovated it with a new hung ceiling that obliterated
the upper row of clerestory windows, in the original dining room. Shepley
Bulfinch Richardson and Abbott cleverly redesigned the ceiling to utilize the
spaces between the roof trusses, thus adding natural light to this already
magnificent space. The new roofs to the adjacent courtyards below are
crenellated to allow views out from the upper part of Main. The mechanical
system, designed to recirculate the heat from the lighting back into the

interior spaces, reflects the 1970s trend toward a general conservation of energy.

The location of the new College Center along what used to be the service side of Main would influence the future development of the adjacent landscape and renovated mechanical spaces to the east, focusing the campus activities away from the front interior of Main to the back and eastern side of this historic building.

2. President's House

Rossiter & Wright, 1895

Completing the circle of buildings around the great lawns to the front of Main is the President's House. Built by the trustees as a gift for President Taylor in honor of his tenth anniversary at Vassar, the house was paid for with funds bequeathed to the college by John Guy Vassar, Matthew Vassar's nephew.[8] President Taylor had campaigned for the construction of faculty housing across Raymond Avenue off the campus itself.[9] This allowed the male faculty and their families to move out of Main into more spacious and more private quarters. With the gift of the President's House, Taylor himself was also able to move out of the undoubtedly claustrophobic atmosphere of Main, as he orchestrated the college's expansion into more modern and spacious facilities scattered across the campus.

Rossiter & Wright, a firm based in New York known largely for its domestic buildings, designed "not a cottage but a dignified,

President's House

well-constructed mansion," to use Rossiter's words.[10] Built in a late-medieval-revival style, the President's House set the tone for the rest of the buildings that came to define the great lawns in front of Main. Its many gables and chimneys, finials and bay windows contrasted sharply with the symmetrical massing of Main to its north. Built of Flemish bond brick with sandstone trim, the President's House also stands out due to its lighter material and more patterned surfaces.

Sarah Gibson Blanding, a champion of modern architecture at Vassar, did not find the dark, fussy ornament of the interior to her liking. She had the stained glass, false ceiling beams, and ornate fireplace of the entry hall removed and then lightened the interior by painting the walnut woodwork white.[11]

3.   Vassar Chapel

Shepley Rutan and Coolidge, 1904

The magnificent Vassar Chapel stands at the southwestern corner of the spacious lawns in front of Main. Although Vassar was non-sectarian from its founding, daily chapel attendance was compulsory until the presidency of Henry Noble MacCracken (1915–46). The college's original chapel occupied the third and fourth floors of Main's rear wing and held six hundred people.[12] It functioned as the major assembly hall for lectures and concerts as well as religious services. Like the rest of the buildings framing the lawn, the construction of a new building for the chapel represents the increasing

Vassar Chapel

decentralization of Vassar life as the college outgrew the original Main
Building.

The new chapel is a Norman revival structure that seats fourteen
hundred people. The architects, Shepley Rutan and Coolidge, a distinguished Boston firm, were heirs to the well-known Romanesque revival
architect Henry Hobson Richardson.[13] All three partners were working for
Richardson at the time of his death at which point they formed their own
practice and completed the unfinished projects from Richardson's office.
This second-generation firm was well known for its Romanesque revival
design of the Stanford University campus in 1892.[14] By the time they
received the Vassar Chapel commission in 1902, the architects had used a
wide range of architectural styles. Originally designing a Gothic revival
chapel for Vassar, they reworked their plan after the college rejected the first
scheme as too large for the available site. They introduced a Romanesque
style for the chapel's exterior using typically Norman forms such as the
chevron molding to decorate the arches of the groin-vaulted portico and the
rose window of the facade. The clear articulation of the large apse to the
rear and transepts lends the chapel the sense of mass and simplicity characteristic of the Romanesque style. The asymmetrical placement of the tower,
which holds the chaplain's offices, is typical of Romanesque revival architecture rather than its medieval prototypes. Composed of Cape Ann granite
with Ohio sandstone trim, the yellow and brown tones of the exterior are
consistent with Taylor Hall to the chapel's north.

The interior is spacious and open, articulated by different stylistic
sources from its exterior. The angel-headed hammerbeam ceiling is reminiscent of English Gothic parish churches. The rich tones of the stained-
glass windows also recall Gothic churches. Renowned stained-glass artist
John La Farge designed the west nave windows to take advantage of the
evening light—the translucent pur-
ple and gold glass glows with the
rays of the setting sun. Louis
Comfort Tiffany, the other major
stained-glass artist of the day,
designed the windows on the east
side of the nave to exploit the bright
early morning light. Tiffany is also
responsible for the rose window so
memorable for its subtle gradations
of white to blue glass. Robert
Leftwich Dodge, a follower of
Tiffany and La Farge, designed the

OPPOSITE: *Vassar Chapel, interior*
THIS PAGE: *Vassar Chapel, Tiffany rose window*

LEFT: *Vassar Chapel, stained-glass windows designed by La Farge*
RIGHT: *Vassar Chapel, stained-glass windows designed by Tiffany*

windows on either side of the organ. All three designers, La Farge, Tiffany, and Dodge, are renowned for their innovations in glass production, which created new effects in light and color as well as for the beauty of their designs.[15]

Many of the windows were donated as class gifts with others coming from individual alumnae. The trustees donated the lovely Tiffany rose window in 1906 in honor of President Taylor's twenty years of service to the college.[16] The chapel itself was the gift of Mary Morris Pratt (Vassar 1877), wife of trustee Charles M. Pratt, and her close friend Mary Thaw Thompson (Vassar 1880).[17] Upon the completion of the chapel, Vassar's trustees declared the great lawns off-limits to further development, thus preserving the stately approach to Main through Taylor gate.

4. Frances Lehman Loeb Art Center

Cesar Pelli & Associates; Balmori Associates, Landscape Architects, 1994

The principal donor for this art gallery, which was completed in 1994, was Frances Lehman Loeb (Vassar 1928), a former Vassar trustee (1988–96) and a patron of the arts. The donors for the sculpture garden accompanying the building were Jane Baker Nord (Vassar 1949) and Eric Nord. The entry pavilion was named in honor of Blanchette Hooker Rockefeller (Vassar 1931) by her family.

The history of the art gallery originated in 1865 when Matthew Vassar donated the Magoon Collection of Art to be located in Main Building.

It consisted of over four hundred works of art including a wonderful collection of Hudson River School paintings. The collection has grown to comprise over 16,000 works of art spanning time periods from ancient Egypt to the present. The museum's current home includes 30,000 square feet of new space. In addition, Cesar Pelli renovated 30,000 square feet of space from the former Vassar College Art Gallery located in Taylor Hall for the use of the art history department.

In the mid-nineties, educational institutions built many new and renovated museum facilities around the country. John Morris Dixon, former editor of *Progressive Architecture* magazine, wrote in an article on the subject:

> Architecturally, the campus museum must actually address a lot of institutional objectives. Internally, it must provide a teaching environment, a venue for the temporary shows, an inducement for art donors, and a setting for receptions. Externally, it must enhance a revered setting yet establish a strong individual identity.[18]

The site for Vassar's new gallery, adjacent to the entrance of the college, was clearly a difficult one, limited by the desire to preserve the long-established chapel walk while creating a special entry for the new museum. The building is located along Raymond Avenue, which gives spatial enclosure to the lawn space between Main, the chapel, and Taylor Hall. Once inside the main gate, the visitor is immediately confronted with the all-glass hexagonal entry pavilion that sits in front of the beloved facade of

Frances Lehman Loeb Art Center

Taylor Hall. This entry leads to a glass corridor that connects to the main body of the museum, which includes classrooms, galleries, offices, and an outdoor sculpture garden. The exterior materials of the art center are varied depending on their location, with a pink limestone colonnade framing the entry pavilion and walkway, while the main body of the museum is clad with a limestone base and red-orange colored brick.

Its architect, Cesar Pelli, was born and educated in Argentina, and emigrated to the United States in 1952. From 1954–64 Pelli worked for Eero Saarinen (Noyes House), and from 1968–76 he worked as a design partner for Gruen Associates. He formed his own firm, Cesar Pelli & Associates (based in New Haven, Connecticut), in 1977. That same year he began his deanship at Yale's School of Architecture (1977–86).

Pelli has described himself as a "pragmatist," an architect whose work reflects an allegiance to the specific setting and the building typology expressed, rather than a specific or consistent aesthetic expression:

> For me it is more important to connect with the purpose of the building and the real place where the building is. This means that the images of my buildings must vary to suit their specific circumstances.[19]

This statement helps to account for the wide range of expressions in the large body of Pelli's work to date. In his early project, the Pacific Design Center (1975), nicknamed the "Blue Whale," Pelli used opaque blue ceramic glass to enclose an unusually shaped volume. In the 1980s, he became well known for his residential and commercial tower buildings around the world, such as the Museum of Modern Art Residential Tower (1984) in New York, the World Financial Center Towers in Battery Park City (1987), and the more recent Petronas Towers in Kuala Lumpur. One of Pelli's first institutional buildings was Herring Hall at Rice University where he was charged with adding a new structure to the historic fabric of the Ralph Adams Cram buildings. As John Pastier has written,

> The commission for Herring Hall, Rice's business school, produced a superbly thought-out building that may be the most intellectually substantial postmodern design in the country.[20]

At Rice, Pelli's postmodern vocabulary navigated between his earlier modernist training and his appreciation for historical architecture. This project would begin a new body of institutional work, similar in nature, to which Vassar's museum is closely related.

The interior of the Lehman Loeb Art Center incorporates a renovated portion of Taylor Hall, including classrooms, offices, slide and photography rooms, and a library. The curved glass passageway that links Taylor to the new building opens into a rectangular lobby. On its right is the main gallery space displaying works from the permanent collection; on the left

Diana Moore, Large Red Head, *1986.*
Gift of William Beckman, 2000

are the prints and drawings galleries, a three-room suite for works on paper, and an open stairway leading to the second floor. The second floor holds offices, classrooms, and a seminar room with special lighting conditions, where any work from the collection can be brought for students to examine.

The primary gallery space is elegantly proportioned and detailed. Its square modules can be reconfigured to accommodate different exhibition conditions. Columns, floor patterns, and an effective ceiling section that includes a clerestory for natural lighting, make up these square bays. The floor pattern, made of end-cut Douglas fir bordered by antique long-leaf pine, provides a warm contrast to the white walls of the gallery.

A lovely sculpture garden designed by landscape architect Diana Balmori, a former partner of Cesar Pelli who formed her own landscape firm of Balmori Associates in 1990, and coauthor of *The American Lawn,*[21] is located to the west of the main galleries along Raymond Avenue, between Taylor and the museum. This garden, designed to hold outdoor sculptures, is also used for special events related to the museum and the college. A large storage space is included in the building's basement, which allows students access to the works of art not on display, thus complementing the teaching mission of the college. The Frances Lehman Loeb Art Center is a tribute to Vassar's long and distinguished history of art program and to its well-known art collection.

5. Kendrick House

York & Sawyer, 1927

Located just across from the college's main gate, Kendrick House represents Vassar's long tradition of housing its faculty as well as its students. For most women faculty members, who were originally obliged to live side by side with the students in Main Building, college housing was a burdensome economic necessity that lacked privacy. As new residence halls were built

Kendrick House

and women faculty were no longer required to supervise student behavior, a greater range of housing choices was developed for them. Kendrick is an early example of faculty housing for women built off-campus (albeit just barely) that provided greater privacy but also the opportunity for companionship through communal dining similar to that found in the student residence halls.

Money for the building's construction and an endowment for its maintenance were given by Myra Avery, sister of Georgia Avery Kendrick, the college's lady principal for twenty-two years. In her will, Miss Avery stated that she wished to donate "a visible memorial of my sister's...many years of devoted service."[22] Initially, the donor expressed a preference for a colonial revival building, but President MacCracken dissuaded her from that choice, suggesting in a letter to Myra Avery that "The proximity of the building to the medieval architecture of Taylor Hall and the chapel would seem to involve a somewhat earlier type of architecture than American colonial."[23]

One of several richly detailed medieval revival gems built under President MacCracken, Kendrick House's style and materials are clearly similar to Blodgett Hall, another York & Sawyer project at Vassar of the same time. Stone for Kendrick was purchased from the nearby Harrison quarry, which closely matched that used for nearby Taylor Hall.[24] The medieval domestic vocabulary, proportions, and U-shaped plan are reminiscent of Wimpfheimer Nursery School, also completed in 1927. Leaded windows, gabled roofs, dormers, balconies, and chimneys all suggest a cozy domestic interior with an interesting variety of rooms.

Indeed, Kendrick offered its residents a choice of living arrangements: single rooms with shared kitchenettes and either shared or private bathrooms, and small one- to two-bedroom apartments with private kitchenettes and baths were available for faculty housing on the first and second floors.[25] Rooms for the housekeepers and maids were located on the third floor. Miss Avery wished to provide affordable housing for faculty members, particularly those at lower salary levels, and they were consulted extensively during the building's design about what kind of room arrangements would suit their needs as well as their budgets. Kendrick was planned for single female faculty; the larger units were intended for those who wished to share a space with each other or with female family members, often mothers or sisters for whom they were responsible. In 1927, the year Kendrick opened, rents ranged from $294 to $770 per annum and averaged $300 (without room service during the summer).[26]

The somewhat cramped quarters of the private living spaces were compensated for by the richly detailed public rooms located on the first floor. These had dark wooden wainscoting with ornate plaster ceilings in keeping with the late-medieval style of the exterior. The dining room, which served meals to all faculty residents, also included a stone fireplace and hearth. The common entrance hall, lounge, and dining room created an opportunity for companionship through limited communal living. The provision of housekeeping services and meals acknowledged the difficulty of accomplishing domestic tasks while maintaining an academic career.

Kendrick has undergone several changes during its history, including a four-year period (1970–74) when it served as the African-American Cultural Center and student residence building. In 1974 New York State, however, ordered the closing of the building as a dormitory intended primarily (although not exclusively) for African-American students.[27] The state ruled that the dormitory functioned as segregated housing since very few white students chose to live in it. Since then, Kendrick has returned to its use as faculty housing. Its interior has been renovated to provide private apartments rather than the quasi-communal living arrangements of the original plan.

6. Taylor Hall

Allen & Collens, 1915

Visitors to Vassar originally entered through an elegant Second Empire gatehouse aligned with the center of Main Building (see p. 14). Renwick designed this matching gatehouse with a wide central arch for vehicular access and two smaller openings for pedestrians.[28] The original lodge

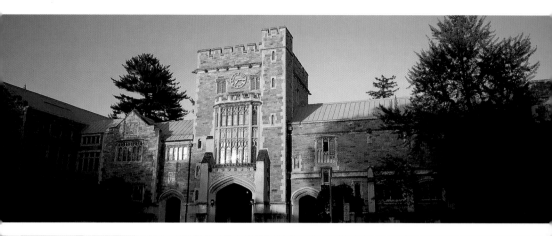

TOP: *Taylor Hall, front facade*
MIDDLE: *Taylor Hall, gate*
BOTTOM: *Taylor Hall, interior*

accommodated the gatekeeper and his family in the apartment housed in its south tower and another employee and his family, originally the college engineer—the aptly named Mr. Gatehouse—on the north side. Its window forms, mansard roofs, and corner pilasters, as well as its brick and slate construction, provide a suitable prologue for the more monumental Main Building beyond. In 1913 the original Renwick gatehouse was demolished and replaced by Taylor Hall.

This Gothic revival building, designed by Allen & Collens, draws on similar English Gothic sources as their earlier design for Thompson Library to the north. Originally, the two were entirely separate structures; in 1937 they were joined together with the addition of Van Ingen Hall. Although Taylor Hall is built of warm golden stone rather than the gray stone of the library, Taylor uses the same Indiana limestone for its elaborately carved trim. Carvings of artists, Athena's owl, and the wolf of Rome, decorate the building's exterior.[29] Like the library, Taylor also features a central crenellated tower. Its large windows filled with Perpendicular-style tracery rise over the rib-vaulted entrance to the college below. Following the same composition as Renwick's original gate, two narrower pedestrian entrances flank the wide arch of the main entrance with a gatekeeper's lodge originally housed on the north side. In addition to acting as the college gatehouse, Taylor was also designed to house Vassar's renowned art department and museum collections. The southern wing of the building contains the main lecture hall for the art department, home to Vassar's renowned art survey course. Each seat is equipped with a tiny light to facilitate note-taking in the dark.

The Vassar art collection, now housed in the Frances Lehman Loeb Art Center to the south of Taylor Hall, was once located in the gallery space above the Taylor Hall gatehouse. The growing art collection had moved from Main to Avery Hall (then called the Museum) in 1875 with the college's natural history collections and then to Taylor Hall in 1915. In both Avery and the new galleries at Taylor, original artworks were displayed together with casts and photographs as a study collection for the art department. In 1922 the casts were removed, and the galleries became the home exclusively to original works of art from the college's collection as well as loan exhibitions. Classes in studio art, suspended upon the death of Professor Van Ingen in 1898, were re-established when Taylor Hall opened in 1915.[30]

Mr. and Mrs. Charles Pratt gave the building to Vassar in honor of James Monroe Taylor, Vassar's fourth president. At the dedication, on Founder's Day, 1915, President Emeritus Taylor spoke of Vassar's early emphasis on the serious study of art. Several early trustees, including Elias Magoon, well-known engraver Benson Lossing, and Samuel F. B. Morse, well known as a painter as well as the inventor of the telegraph, were leading members of the art world. Still, following the model of contemporary male institutions, Vassar's original trustees were hesitant to include music

Frederick F. Thompson Memorial Library with Martha Rivers and E. Bronson Ingram Library addition at far right

and art in the regular curriculum, offering both as special courses available for an extra fee and a separate degree. Taylor himself was responsible for making music and art part of Vassar's college curriculum with the same rigorous standards found in other departments.

7.   Frederick F. Thompson Memorial Library

> *Allen & Collens, 1905; wings Allen & Collens, 1918;*
> *renovations: Hardy Holzman Pfeiffer Associates, 2001*

Van Ingen Hall

> *Allen, Collens & Willis with Theodore Muller and John McAndrew, 1937;*
> *renovation, Shepley and Bulfinch, 1963*

Helen Lockwood addition

> *Hellmuth, Obata and Kassabaum, 1977*

Martha Rivers and E. Bronson Ingram Library addition

> *Hardy Holzman Pfeiffer Associates, 2001*

The first of many phases of library construction on this site, the original section of the Thompson Library established a Gothic prototype for development along this part of Raymond Avenue. Vassar's library, like most of its facilities, had originally been housed in Main Building where it rapidly outgrew its small thirty-by-thirty-five-foot room opposite the chapel.[31] Reluctant to build a separate structure that would force students to leave Main for evening study, trustee Frederick Thompson donated money for the annex, known as Uncle Fred's Nose, built at the front of Main in 1893, to house the growing library. This solution proved short-lived; the rapid overcrowding of the annex was relieved by the donation of an entirely new and separate library by Thompson's generous widow, Mary Clark Thompson.[32]

Thompson Memorial Library, with its elaborate window traceries and finely carved pinnacles, offers a delicate counterpoint to Main, Renwick's massive Second Empire monument across the lawn. Drawing on the English Perpendicular period of Gothic, the medieval vocabulary of Thompson contrasts sharply with the simpler Tudor or Elizabethan forms found elsewhere at Vassar. The crenellated and turreted central entrance way resembles a medieval castle gate while the central tower standing behind is reminiscent of ecclesiastical architecture with its long trefoil lancets and crocketed pinnacles. Built primarily of Germantown stone and trimmed in ornately carved Indiana limestone, this majestic facade opens into one of Vassar's most memorable spaces.[33] The entrance hall formed by the tower's interior is lit by the clerestory windows located high above the open tracery panel screens, tapestries, and carved square panels decorating the stone walls. The navelike space that extends back from the entrance hall with transeptlike wings to the north and south reinforces the library's ecclesiastical quality. A massive stained-glass window depicting the first woman to receive a doctorate, Elena Lucrezia Cornaro Piscopia, defending her dissertation in 1678, dominates the main interior space of the original library. Her costume of gray and rose satin, the college's original colors, symbolizes the dawn of women's higher education at Vassar. A. W. Pugin's grandson Dunstan Powell designed the window, which has become an emblem of Vassar's original educational mission. Other leaded windows found throughout this part of the library contain depictions of fifteenth- and sixteenth-century printers' symbols.

Thompson Library, interior

Mrs. Thompson went on to fund the wings added to the north and south of the original library in 1918.[33] These wings, built in the same style as the original library, formed interior courtyards once used as outdoor reading rooms by students.

By 1924 plans were again under way for the library's further expansion. In 1935, after fourteen different sets of plans had been considered, Charles Collens of Allen, Collens and Willis designed the Van Ingen addition, which connected Taylor to the original library.[34] This addition is named for Henry Van Ingen, professor of art at Vassar from 1865–98. The Van Ingen Library, located on the north side of Taylor Hall, expanded the home of the art department and provided additional stack space for the main library on its first three floors with a new art library housed above. Van Ingen's top floor holds a drafting room for architecture students, a lecture hall, a conference room, and offices.[37] A set of corridors, lined with a map room, library offices, conference rooms, faculty studies, and seminar rooms for various departments, served as the connection between the two buildings. Designed by Theodore Muller of New York and Professor John McAndrew, a member of the art department and curator of the architecture department of the Museum of Modern Art in New York, the interiors are frankly modern in their design. The space is articulated with glass block partition walls and modern details. The exterior of this addition preserves the overall proportions and forms of the original Gothic revival buildings to either side, but with a more simplified decorative vocabulary.

Despite the art library's modern interior, the much beloved Gothic vocabulary of the exterior was preserved in this and the next revision of the Thompson Library. In 1959 the firm of Shepley Bulfinch Richardson and Abbott was hired to carry out a new phase of additions and alterations. The architects' program included improvements to the circulation system and

TOP: *Leaded windows with fifteenth- and sixteenth-century printers' symbols*
OPPOSITE: *Thompson Library, interior*

LEFT: *Martha Rivers and E. Bronson Ingram*
Library Addition, Class of 1951 Reading Room
RIGHT: *Thompson Library, view of Media Cloisters*

the addition of new library space while also preserving the Gothic design of the original building and leaving its exterior unchanged. They inserted new stairways at the center of the building joined to glass bridges connecting the upper floors without obscuring the view of the famous stained-glass windows. Additional library space was gained by filling in the courtyard areas of the earlier building. The basement was completely modernized as well, adding both study and stack space to the library.

In 1977 the Lockwood addition by Hellmuth, Oban and Kassabaum was added to the north side of Thompson along Raymond Avenue, sponsored by a generous gift from Helen Lockwood and other Vassar alumnae/i. Lockwood (Vassar 1912) had been a member of the English department from 1927–56. This 32,000-square-foot addition contained the Francis Fitz Randolph Rare Book Room, gift of Francis Fitz Randolph, a former trustee and patron of the arts, as well as a new reserve room, an all-night study lounge, additional stack areas, and faculty carrels. The concrete facade was the architect's second proposal after their all-glass facade had been rejected in favor of the more solid-looking building, still partly visible from the Raymond Avenue entrance gate. The neutral quality of this addition to Thompson was effective in allowing the historic neo-Gothic facade of Thompson to remain the prominent piece of the library complex.

The latest addition to Thompson Library is the Martha Rivers and E. Bronson Ingram Library named in honor of its principal donor, Martha Rivers Ingram (Vassar 1957) and in memory of her late husband, E. Bronson

Martha Rivers and E. Bronson Ingram Library addition

Ingram. It was completed in 2001 by Hardy Holzman Pfeiffer Associates. This established architecture and interior design firm, which came to recognition in the 1960s for its innovative high-tech vocabulary, has evolved into a major practice. Today their firm is widely known for its institutional work, especially in the area of theater design and historic restoration. They have successfully completed several restorations of such notables as the New Victory and New Amsterdam theaters in New York as well as new performing arts buildings including the Dance Theatre of Harlem's Everett Center. Their Los Angeles Public Library building of 1993 represents a project of similar challenges to that of Vassar's library including a master plan for the new complex, a new addition, and a restoration of a historic library building.

The Martha Rivers and E. Bronson Ingram Library added 30,000 new square feet to the old library complex and literally wraps a layer of space all around the earlier Lockwood facade, culminating in a new reading room at the north end of the building. This highly textured facade incorporates materials from neighboring buildings in order to give it a contextual reading. The mottled limestone base creates a frame for the upper facade, which is articulated with red and burgundy bricks configured in a diamond-shape composition and completed with a standing seam copper roof.

The master plan for the new complex has successfully clarified the intricate circulation systems that had evolved over years of renovations and additions to the existing Thompson and Lockwood libraries. A long central north–south corridor now connects the Van Ingen addition to the Thompson

Rockefeller Hall

Library and finally to the new north wing. Here, the new facility provides reserve and periodical rooms, information resource rooms and equipment, study spaces and a reading room as well as a new center for the Vassar College Archives and Special Collections. The interior is plainly detailed except for the richly decorated Class of 1951 Reading Room at the north end of the building.

Hugh Hardy's 2001 renovations to the Thompson Library preserved the architectural elements and the scholarly aura that make Thompson one of the most admired buildings on campus, while greatly expanding electronic infrastructure and facilities for research and teaching, and simplifying navigation through the space. Of particular note are the Media Cloisters, the new technology center on the second floor of Thompson. In an open space defined by Gothic arches, with a spectacular view of the Cornaro window, high-end computer equipment is available to the entire community for individual or collaborative projects.

8. Rockefeller Hall

York & Sawyer, 1897; Enlarged 1916, 1940

Vassar's first general academic building provided much-needed space for class lectures as well as individual consultation with faculty members. Before this building's construction, faculty members had resorted to renting student sitting rooms in order to hold private meetings with students.[36] With the addition of Rockefeller to the emerging quadrangle, Vassar turned its focus from Main to an expanded college campus with more professional and modern facilities. Donated by John D. Rockefeller, the commission for the building was awarded through an architectural competition. Edward York and Philip Sawyer, employees of McKim, Mead & White, submitted a scheme that Sawyer had designed for a high school in Plainfield, New Jersey.[37] Admiring the general plan, President Taylor requested that the architects modify the elevation to make it look more collegiate. After reviewing examples of English architecture, York redrew the facade and won the commission, with an impressive construction budget of $100,000. With this commission, York & Sawyer began what became one of the most successful and prestigious practices of American architectural firms in the early twentieth century, as well as a long association with Vassar.

York's review of English building examples led him to a rather eclectic design for Rockefeller Hall. Many of its features, such as the large multi-paned windows and gabled roofline, are clearly drawn from late-medieval English sources. Tudor or Elizabethan models were favored for college buildings of the time as their large windows provided the light necessary for the classrooms. At Rockefeller, these forms are combined with other features more often associated with Georgian architecture such as the prominent fan light and columns of the central entrance. The semicircular apse projecting from the rear of the building houses large lecture spaces amply lit by the many close-set windows. The visual division of the front facade into three principal units is articulated by the gables found over each of the wings and central entrance. Limestone quoins at the corners of these units lend them further emphasis as they project slightly from the rest of the facade. The bold use of limestone and sculptural details of the principal entrance and wings enlivens the facade of Rockefeller Hall. The building's two principal stories are raised up on a high English basement, also lit by large Tudoresque windows. The basement is differentiated from the rest of the elevation by its use of limestone striping and separated from the first floor with a continuous stone string course.

The renovations of 1916 added space for offices and seminar rooms and also improved the building's ventilation and acoustics. The attic was renovated in 1940 to create additional space for teaching and offices.[38]

Chicago Hall

9.   Chicago Hall

Schweikher and Elting, 1959

Chicago Hall opened in 1959, built for the French, German, Spanish, Italian, and Russian departments. (In 1935 Vassar was the first women's college in the nation to introduce Russian into the curriculum.) The building, named after its Chicago alumnae donors, is one of Vassar's modern gems and an excellent example of the 1950s American modern style. In 1954 Eero Saarinen's master plan for the north end of the campus designated this site for Chicago Hall. The building became the southern boundary of the large lawn framed by the quad dormitories, Josselyn House, and Raymond Avenue.

The architects of the new language building were Paul Schweikher and Winston Elting. Paul Schweikher had established his reputation as an avant-garde designer when his work was exhibited in the 1933 landmark exhibition on modern architecture at the Museum of Modern Art in New York. Winston Elting later joined Schweikher in a partnership that became known for its exploration of new building materials and technologies, particularly in the postwar period. In the mid-fifties Schweikher became the chair of architecture at Yale and later headed the Department of Architecture at Carnegie Mellon Institute. Chicago Hall was Schweikher and Elting's last commission together and is one of their most celebrated works.

Just as Noyes and Ferry houses (see pp. 89 and 148) creatively interpret their sites, Chicago's design established its own original relationship to the landscape. When viewed from Josselyn House, its graceful horizontal facade seen against a backdrop of majestic trees and the library tower beyond, was a convincing architectural statement in spite of Chicago's modest size.

Chicago Hall has a distinctive relationship to the ground plane. The structure is placed on a continuous concrete rectangular base elevated approximately twelve inches above the ground plane; it was once sur-rounded by a border of fine gravel stone, making it look like an island in the landscape. This thoughtful progression from the campus landscape into the building can be read as a symbolic journey into another world, into the realm of other languages. In fact, students were expected to speak only in foreign languages while in this building. The main entrance, located in the middle of the south facade, is a three-bay concrete vaulted space connected to a one-bay central corridor on axis with the entry to Josselyn House. The Weyerhaeuser Auditorium and three classroom/office wings, organized by languages, are staggered off this central hallway, separated by courtyard gardens. This configuration, with its clear reference to Japanese architec-ture, allows a garden view for all of the offices and classrooms while main-taining an intimate learning environment and a sense of a shared interior community. The plan is reminiscent of the firm's earlier work in Chicago such as the Rockwell House (1956) and the First Universalist Church (1954). Schweikher and Elting's approach to the inclusion of landscape into the building design differs from Breuer's earlier example at Ferry House. Breuer used the classic modern approach that favors transparency of the exterior facade to incorporate landscape within.

The interplay of solids and voids in Chicago's building plan is unified by the continuous expression of the concrete vaulted roof. Each vault is approximately six feet eight inches in width and becomes a working module in the definitions of the interior spaces. This building design pre-dates Kahn's Kimball Art Museum in Fort Worth (1972), where a similar concept was developed into a more sophisticated expression. At Chicago, the classrooms are generally two bays wide while the faculty offices consti-tute one bay. The interior finishes are expressed as exposed structural ele-ments: the walls are made of concrete block, floors of finished concrete slabs, and the roof of exposed concrete vaults. The exterior courtyard walls consist of single-pane glass with thin metal frames arranged in a staggered double pattern of rectilinear shapes and include some operable portions. This pattern recalls the configuration of the building plan itself. The facade of the former auditorium features a decorative pre-cast double concrete screen wall designed by the sculptor Erwin Hauer, which acts as a light filter by staggering the two planes of concrete openings against one another. As sunlight passes through the wall, it casts a subtle and delicate light into the interior space.

Alumnae House

10. Alumnae House

Hunt & Hunt, 1924; Linda Yowell 1999

Alumnae House stands outside the college walls across Raymond Avenue and is raised high above the campus on a site known as Rock Lot. Built under President MacCracken, Alumnae House's original intention was to offer the opportunity for continuing education and involvement in college life to Vassar alumnae. Although used largely as a guest house with dining open to the public for much of its history, Alumnae House was planned to provide a place of residence for alumnae when they returned to Vassar for educational purposes such as conferences, further study, or meetings with college faculty about ongoing projects.[39] The many school teachers among Vassar alumnae were encouraged to further their education by staying in contact with their alma mater.

The building's architectural vocabulary is closely related to its neighbor, the Williams Faculty Apartment Building, in its use of a half-timbered Tudor revival style. Architects Hunt & Hunt, who also built Williams, were chosen by the building's donors, Blanche Ferry Hooker (Vassar 1894) and Queene Ferry Coonley (Vassar 1896).[40] The slate roof, leaded windows, and medieval revival furnishings are typical of Vassar buildings from this period. A large entrance hall with a stone fireplace leads to a terrace. To the left of the entry, the main lounge is located a few steps below the ground floor, serving as a large reception room. Its majestic proportions are defined by the beautiful beamed wooden ceiling and enhanced by the stone fireplace and large medieval revival painting that continue the Tudor revival theme of the exterior. The dining room with the same decorative vocabulary is to the right of the entrance hall. A more casual restaurant, the Pub, is located at the north end of the building. The Pub, so fondly remembered for its murals depicting Vassar life in the 1940s and painted by Jean Anderson (Vassar 1933), was one of the few alternatives to campus dining for many years. The upper two floors contain guest rooms. The third floor was originally designed as spartan dormitory accommodations with shared bathrooms for thirty-five guests. Double bedrooms with shared bathrooms as well as a sewing room were found on the second floor. Architect Linda Yowell (Vassar 1973) made renovations to the building in 1999 with the addition of an elevator that has made the building handicap-accessible.

The original landscape plan for Alumnae House was designed by the Olmsted Brothers firm, sons of Frederick Law Olmsted. Their careful shaping of the rocky hill in front of the house gave the building a sense of place overlooking the college grounds while also buffering it from the noise of Raymond Avenue.

In the brochure produced to solicit funds for the building's furnishings, President MacCracken wrote of his conception of Alumnae House, "Alumnae House takes its place among our academic buildings as no less an integral part than any of the undergraduate dormitories."[41] The late-medieval domestic architectural style and furnishings tie Alumnae House stylistically to Vassar's early dormitories. It has hosted many conferences, including those for alumnae/i following reunion weekend, as part of its educational mission, echoing MacCracken's ideas about the interrelationship between a Vassar education and the world beyond the college's gates.

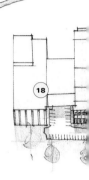

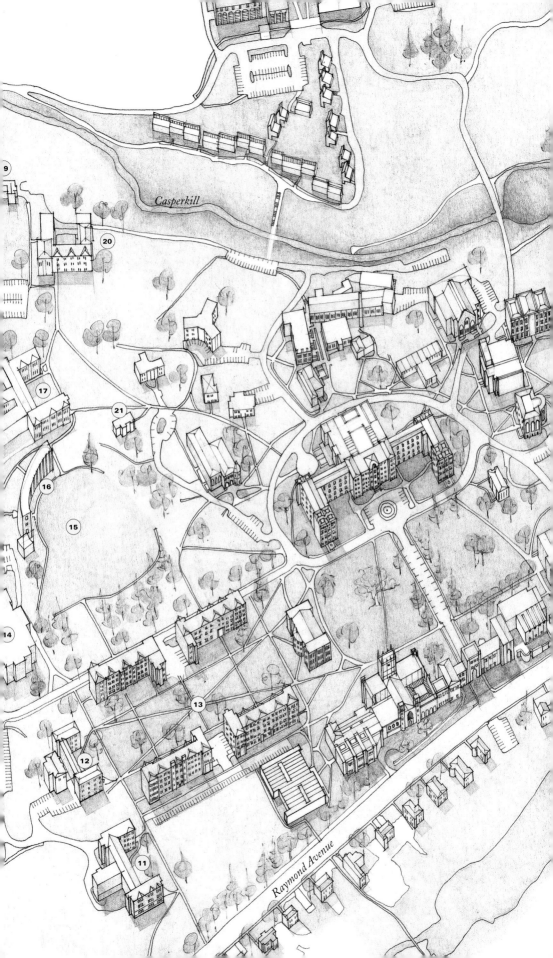

Casperkill

9

20

17

21

16

15

14

13

12

11

Raymond Avenue

Olivia P. Josselyn House

11. Olivia P. Josselyn House

Allen & Collens, 1912

Josselyn House is the last of the six dormitories built under President Taylor, located to the northwest of Main Building. It followed the model of contemporary residential architecture adopted at rival institutions such as Wellesley and Smith in providing a comfortable, homelike setting for its occupants. Josselyn's U-shaped plan follows the orientation of its neighbors, Jewett and the four quadrangle dorms. Its low, wide forms dominate the vast lawns—popularly known as Joss Beach—that once extended beyond the full length of the quadrangle to Thompson Library. Built of rough brick with granite trim, Josselyn follows a late-medieval revival style with leaded casement windows and a slate roof. Both inside and out, its decoration is far more elaborate than that of its neighbors along the quadrangle. At the time of its construction, Josselyn was regarded as luxurious in both its facilities and furnishings, although having the disadvantage of being too distant from the library, chapel, and recitation-classroom buildings. Among the luxuries that delighted students were the college's first dormitory showers. Similar to the residential quarters in Main, small kitchens equipped with running water, a gas stove, and storage space were also included on each floor. These facilities allowed residents to cook at any time and eliminated a major source of untidiness in student rooms. The arrangement of the rooms along lengthy corridors is similar to that found in Jewett although without the much maligned tower of the earlier dormitory.

Josselyn, now accommodating 200 residents, was originally intended to house 120 students in a series of single rooms and two-person suites consisting of two bedrooms and a sitting room. Josselyn's rooms, larger than Jewett's, were also better furnished. Each bedroom featured dark mission-style woodwork with a desk and desk chair, two large armchairs, a bookcase, and a velvet rug. Single rooms were painted pale green and doubles were painted buff. The blankets and other linens were all monogrammed with VC.[42]

The parlor and dining room received particular praise for their successful design and tasteful furnishings. A small hall opposite the middle entrance of the building leads to a pair of doors opening into a huge living room. Wood paneling and a deep, wide fireplace framed by built-in bookcases continue the medieval revival theme of the exterior. Full-length leaded windows occupy almost the entire east and west walls. Mrs. Frederick Thompson, trustee from 1899–1914, provided the original lavish living room furnishings.[43] Oriental rugs covered the floor with a variety of mission-style tables alternating with several deep sofas and a Steinway baby grand piano. One contemporary account in *Vassar Alumnae Magazine* described the effect as, "that of massive luxuriousness and peaceful comfort at the same time."[44] The former dining room features similar decorative details with a large fireplace, over which hung a portrait of Olivia Josselyn, after whom the hall is named. Her daughter, Mrs. Russell Sage, gave Josselyn House in her honor.

Josselyn House, parlor

Jewett House

12. Jewett House

Pilcher & Tachau, 1907; renovation, Herbert S. Newman & Partners, 2003

Originally named "North," Jewett House closed off the north end of the newly built quadrangle. Despite the construction of four dormitories between 1893 and 1902, demand for housing on campus remained strong, so the trustees decided to build Jewett in 1907, the only quad building whose principal facade faces the interior.

Designed by Lewis Pilcher, Vassar art professor and later state architect of New York, Jewett was composed of two distinctly different parts. A U-shaped building of four floors at the front contained the parlors and dining rooms on the ground floor of the central section, opening off the main entrance hall. The remainder of this part of the building held student rooms along long corridors. Attached to the rear of this structure and accessible from it at the ground floor only was a nine-story tower also containing student rooms.

One reason for Jewett's odd proportions is suggested by the 30,000-gallon water tank (now removed) built under the roof of the tower from steel plates on site to improve the college's water pressure. Another innovation discovered during the recent renovation of the building is the extensive use of steel and concrete construction throughout the building, which contains almost no wooden structural elements.

The lighter red brick and terra cotta trim of Jewett resemble those of Rockefeller Hall at the far end of the quadrangle, contrasting with the darker brick and brownstone and the relatively simple stone embellishment on the quad dorms. The elaborate detailing of Jewett, with its capped tower, crenellations, grotesque terra cotta faces, animals, and other late-medieval features, is unlike that of the other quad dorms and was facilitated by Pilcher's very early use of terra cotta instead of stone for these purposes. The inclusion of the tower in Jewett's design created a more monumental and less homelike impression than that of its neighbor, Josselyn. Perhaps this explains Jewett's nickname of "Pilcher's Crime."

Vassar was unable to find a donor for the building, which was constructed with college funds. At the college's fiftieth anniversary in 1915, President MacCracken decided that North should be renamed in honor of Milo P. Jewett, Vassar's first president. Housing 235 students, Jewett is considerably larger than any of its neighboring dormitories. Its renovation in 2002–03 is the first step in the college's master plan for residence halls. Jewett residents now enjoy enhanced living spaces and public areas that are more accessible and conducive to group living.

13. The Vassar quadrangle

Strong House
> *Francis R. Allen, 1893*

Raymond House
> *Francis R. Allen, 1897*

Davison House
> *Allen & Vance, 1902*

Lathrop House
> *Allen & Vance, 1901*

The initial impression of the dark brick dormitories framing the gracious parklike space of the Vassar quadrangle is one of uniformity. Despite their resemblance to one another, Strong, Raymond, Davison, and Lathrop were not planned as a group from the start. Initially, only Strong was planned on the site, easily accessible to Main, the new gym, and classroom buildings. As the Strong model proved successful, discussion turned to how future dormitories could be best arranged. The quadrangle form was reached after some deliberation. Consultant Frederick Olmsted recommended an "echelon arrangement" of buildings forming two diagonal lines widening at the north end to create a greater sense of open space. However, the designers, Francis Allen and the firm of York & Sawyer, architects of Rockefeller Hall, together with Taylor and the trustees chose the more conventional quadrangular composition.[45]

In plan, the dorms, together with Jewett House and Rockefeller Hall at either end, clearly form a rectangular unit. In practice, the sense of integration and enclosure apparent at other collegiate quadrangles such as

TOP: *Strong House*
BOTTOM: *Residential quadrangle*

those at Columbia or Harvard, is absent from the Vassar space for a variety
of reasons. The vast length of the quad with its many trees and shrubs that
screen views across the interior space, works contrary to the sense of an
open yard framed by buildings as is more usual in quadrangle composi-
tions. Each building is in fact separate at Vassar without being connected to
the other dorms by walkways or colonnades as is the case, for example, at
the University of Virginia's Jefferson campus. In addition, the principal
facades and entrances of Rockefeller and the four dormitories are actually
on the outside of the complex and do not face into the quadrangle itself.
Strong was designed to face the gardens located to its east and the center
of the campus at that time. Thus, the quad dorms do not create a closed collegiate community, but instead act as a series of independent units, each
enjoying a view of the parklike landscape in its backyard.

     The construction of four dormitories in less than ten years allowed
Vassar to expand its enrollment and offer a more modern appearance to
potential students. The seminary-like model of one large building housing
all students and most, if not all, college functions was no longer acceptable
by the late nineteenth century. In designing Strong and its successors,
Francis Allen followed the example of dormitories at newer women's colleges such as Smith and Wellesley. As Helen Horowitz has described, the
preferred model for residence halls in the late nineteenth century was basically a large-scale house with common rooms such as parlors clustered
around the entrance.[46] Student rooms were concentrated on the upper
floors with a few located on the ground floor. As at Vassar's quad dorms,
the dining room and kitchen were located off to the side or even in a wing
projecting from the back of the building with servants' quarters above.

     Strong House was the first building designed specifically as a dor-
mitory at Vassar. Built out of dark brick with brownstone trim in a
Tudoresque style, it set the pattern for the later quadrangle dormitories.
Rising from a rusticated stone base, the four principal floors of the building
were intended to house one hundred students chiefly in single rooms, with
some three-room suites available for two students to share.

     The vast facade is broken into three distinct pieces. Each end unit
projects slightly from the central facade and is articulated by a wide gable
roof. Entrances at each end of the building now lead to faculty residences.
The central section of the building is further subdivided with three central
gables and a pair of bay windows marking the main entrance. Dormers project from the roof between the terminal and central gables. Four chimneys
and three cupolas further vary the roofline. Dividing the building's mass
into separate units through the use of slightly projecting wings, bay windows, chimneys, and gables reduced some of the institutional quality of a
large dormitory. An 1896 description of the building, written just three years
after Strong's construction, acknowledges the severity of its facade, which

TOP: *Davison House*
BOTTOM: *Lathrop House*

Raymond House

was softened by ivy plantings: "Before long 'The Strong' will present the picturesque ivied appearance that is the charm of the old building."[47] Early photographs of the parlor with its dominant fireplace and dining room show further use of a late-medieval decorative vocabulary. The original dining room, housed at the north end of the building, had a beamed ceiling, two stories high, in order to reduce noise levels when all one hundred residents ate together. When Strong first opened, students flocked here to escape the din of Main's much larger dining room. A small balcony resembling a minstrels' gallery, which projects from the second-story level, was used for meal-time serenades by the Glee Club.

Strong was an immediate success as a housing option.[48] Within two years, applications for rooms exceeded the available space, so the college continued the expansion of on-campus dormitory space with the construction of Raymond House across the quadrangle from Strong. Raymond's construction was undertaken at the same time as that of Rockefeller Hall, establishing the area to the north of Main as a new locus of Vassar life. Raymond was unique among the four quad dorms in developing a cooperative housing plan as did Blodgett Hall in 1933. Raymond residents received a $115 deduction from their annual bill for performing housekeeping duties in their dormitory. The cooperative living plan was available at Raymond until 1942–43.

In 1901 and 1902 Lathrop and Davison were added to complete the sides of the new quadrangle. The four dormitories are similar in materials and overall form but their details vary. Battlements are used on Lathrop, for example, but not on Strong, cupola details vary, as do chimney shapes and rooflines. Overall, however, the effect is very much that of a harmonious group built in two straight lines along the quadrangle.

Funding for the four dormitories came from a variety of sources. Initially, the college planned to pay for Strong itself but soon realized it lacked adequate funds. President Taylor, a prominent Baptist minister, called on fellow Baptist John D. Rockefeller for help in funding the new dormitory. Taylor, one of Rockefeller's principal advisors, had brought him on to the Vassar Board of Trustees in 1888. Rockefeller's daughter, Bessie Rockefeller Strong, attended Vassar from 1886 to 1888, and her father asked that the new dormitory be named in her honor.[49] In 1902 Rockefeller donated the last of the four buildings, which was named in honor of his mother, Eliza Davison.[50] In between, the college itself paid for Raymond House, named in honor of the college's second president.[51] Lathrop House was also paid for by the college and named after Dr. Edward Lathrop, a charter trustee of Vassar.[52]

14. Students' Building (All Campus Dining Center)

McKim, Mead & White, 1913;
renovation as All Campus Dining Center, Walker O. Cain & Associates, 1973;
renovation, Finegold Alexander+ Associates Inc, 2003

Following the expansion of the college's classroom and dormitory space in the early years of his presidency, Taylor turned toward providing improved facilities for students' recreational and social lives. He first suggested a building specifically for these purposes in 1901. In 1902 the Students'

Students' Building (All Campus Dining Center)

Association was chartered following its reorganization. Overseeing the many student clubs and committees, the association received office space in the Students' Building when it opened in 1913. An anonymous donor, later identified as alumna Mary Babbott Ladd (Vassar 1908), provided the funds and named the new center for student life.[53]

Its large columned portico and pedimented entranceway identify the Students' Building as an example of Southern colonial revival architecture. As with all revivals, the connection with the past is not literal but the use of a columned portico, red brick, and white trim is intended to evoke Jeffersonian domestic architecture on a grander scale. McKim, Mead & White were widely favored as campus architects in the early twentieth century after their many successes at Columbia and New York University as well as the University of Virginia, where their use of Southern colonial revival provided models for the Vassar building. Joseph Herendon Clark, the young architect in charge of this project for McKim, Mead & White, identifies Christ Church in Alexandria, Virginia, attended by George Washington, as the specific source of inspiration for the Students' Building.[54]

The portico led to an elegant foyer at the front of the new building. The original plan featured a large auditorium occupying the central block of the structure.[55] Seating 1,200, the auditorium included a large stage with seating on the ground floor and a gallery that wrapped around the room in a U-shape at second-floor level. The ornate plaster ceiling, ionic gallery columns, and dentil moldings continue the neoclassical vocabulary of the exterior. Large arched windows above the gallery light the interior. The seating arrangement, window forms, and decoration of the original interior were clearly reminiscent of colonial church architecture with the stage replacing the altar and pulpit. Small one-story wings projected from either side of the main auditorium block. These housed meeting rooms for student groups such as Philaletheis, the Vassarion, and the Miscellany. The auditorium provided much needed space for many college activities. Lectures by popular outside speakers could be readily accommodated in the large space, and the floor could be cleared for college dances. The student population had long ago outgrown the parlors provided for socializing and entertaining in Matthew Vassar's Main Building. In 1945 the Students' Building was refurbished with added space for a new student snack bar, known as "The Hoot."[56]

In 1968, with the advent of coeducation, the college decided to consolidate all dining facilities in one location, ending the tradition of dining in the halls of residence. This decision was primarily influenced by the economic inefficiency of separate dining halls. Over the years, various proposals were developed for the consolidation of campus dining, including one that placed a dining hall in the center of the quadrangle and linked it by footbridges to the surrounding dormitories. In 1970 the college decided to renovate and expand the Students' Building to serve as the new dining center. The family and friends of the original donor, Mary Ladd, provided funds for the rebuilding.[57] The building's exterior changed as the one-story wings were greatly enlarged, altering their relationship to the large central portion. Built of the same materials as the original structure, the wings reveal their more recent date by the modern style of their large windows. The interior was more dramatically altered. Beyond the original lobby is a space for preparing and serving food. The wings to the left and right hold a number of dining spaces of various sizes in an effort to recreate some of the intimacy of the old house dining rooms. The second floor contained a dishwashing facility, a bakery, offices, and staff changing rooms.

The recent second-level restoration by Finegold Alexander + Associates Inc. returns many of its original functions to the Students' Building. Removing the washing, baking, changing, and office space, the project inserts a mezzanine and main floor facility that will serve a wide variety of student needs, from quiet alcoves for study to space for performances and gatherings of up to six hundred people. Offices, media space, a catering kitchen, bathrooms, and a mezzanine café under the restored Adam plaster ceiling will recapture the building's original purpose as a center for student activities.

15. Noyes Circle

1864

Noyes Circle with Emma Hartman Noyes House to the left

The Noyes Circle we see today dates back to the founding of the college. One of the earliest maps of the campus indicates that there were originally three circles in this general location; the two smaller ones were labeled "playgrounds." All of the circles were used for the purpose of exercise, which was so important to Matthew Vassar's notion of a complete education. The large circle had a diameter of approximately five hundred feet, the same dimension as the length of Main Building, and was surrounded by a road and planted hedges, presumably to protect the young women from outside onlookers. This circle was used for both walking and riding, which may explain its very formal configuration in spite of the prevalent garden vocabulary at Vassar of irregular picturesque shapes. Dr. Alida Avery, an early professor of physiology and hygiene, used the circle for her classes and later helped to organize the Floral Society in which students cared for the garden themselves, turning exercise into a useful and aesthetic mission.

The Circle was also the site of the first field day for women in America, held on November 9, 1895. Despite "unpropitious weather," it was laid out for track events, and the students competed in the 100-yard dash, the running broad jump, the running jump, and the 220-yard dash.[58]

16. Emma Hartman Noyes House

Eero Saarinen & Associates, 1958;
parlor restoration, Leonard Parker Associates, 2000

Completed in 1958, Noyes House was Sarah Blanding's second building project, which not only gave vertical dimension to the Circle but also added to the development of contemporary architecture at the college. The discussion of building a new student residence began early in Blanding's presidency as a result of the postwar increase in enrollment. The Noyes family (Katherine F. Noyes, Vassar 1908) gave a major donation to name the new building in honor of their mother Emma Hartman Noyes (Vassar 1880). In 1954 Eero Saarinen had developed a master plan for the north end of the campus. As part of this plan, Saarinen had proposed two crescent-shaped residential buildings to be placed around the Circle. Though only one of them was built, the project reinvigorated this historic site at the college.

By the 1950s, Eero Saarinen had become a well-established architect with a growing practice in large-scale public and institutional projects. Emblematic of an emerging global culture, his work encompassed an evolving set of expressionistic designs, often using sculptural forms to articulate his vision. His work would anticipate many of the mannered developments of late-twentieth-century architecture. Eero's father, Eliel, was a prominent Finnish architect who moved his family to America after winning second prize in the Chicago Tribune Tower Competition. He later designed the Cranbrook Academy and Campus (Detroit) where Eero spent his precocious, design-oriented childhood. As a young architect, Eero apprenticed in his father's firm until 1948 when he won the Jefferson Western Expansion Memorial Competition in St. Louis (better known as the St. Louis Arch), competing against his own father. Eero later credited his father with his theory that one should design in "the next largest context—a chair in a room, a room in a house, a house in an environment, an environment in a city plan."[59] This perspective can be seen in the design of Noyes House and its careful integration into the existing landscape of the Circle, respectful of the site's history as well as its relation to the larger campus.

When he began work on Noyes, Saarinen had already finished the Kresge Auditorium and Chapel at MIT, and was designing the IBM Complex in Yorktown, New York, with which Noyes shares many formal similarities. Noyes is placed along the northeastern section of the Circle so that its

principal facade faces southwest and gestures not only to the circular garden but also to the heart of the college, Main Building. The building's curved plan and its insertion in the landscape create a unique relationship to the site. Vertical brick piers in between the projecting window bays suggest but do not imitate the traditional Gothic style employed in many other buildings at Vassar. The brick piers give the appearance of rising directly out of the earth while the projecting window volumes float above the ground plane suggesting a delicate balance between the two. The rapport with the ground plane is further accentuated by the organic concrete stair structures that spring from below and barely touch the building enclosure.

The facade is made of uneven "hard-burned" brick with black mortar, interrupted by the vertical aluminum-clad window strips. Constructed of poured-in-place concrete, the building houses 156 students, with double rooms on the front, singles along the back, and two house-fellow apartments at the east end of the ground floor. The articulation of the bay windows reflects not only the force of the inward-bending shape but also lends vertical expression to the building. The garden rooms benefit from this projection: a bay window and seat expand their living spaces into the garden beyond. As in Ferry House, the double rooms have been carefully designed to accommodate two people with built-in furniture and cabinetry that divide the room into two spaces, one for study and one for sleeping. The long curved interior corridor, with its two open-ended views to the gardens beyond, brings the landscape into the heart of the residence.

The most memorable interior space of the building is the famous "passion pit," more recently dubbed the "Jetsons' Lounge," located in the ground-floor parlor. This sunken circular seating area is depressed into the floor slab, creating a dialog between the intimate interior seating

ABOVE: *Emma Hartman Noyes House, parlor, called the Jetsons' Lounge*
OPPOSITE: *Emma Hartman Noyes House*

arrangement and the ground plane vista into the landscape. Many poetry readings and small performances have been staged here over the years. The surrounding living room includes Saarinen's well-known furniture. In an interview, architect Gunnar Birkets, who had worked for Saarinen, recalled him saying, "We have four-legged chairs, we have three-legged chairs and I have seen two-legged chairs. So we are going to build a one-legged chair, right?"[60] The freestanding furniture in the living room is known as the Tulip Pedestal Series produced by Knoll Associates in 1956.

The north end of the ground floor contained the house dining room, which has subsequently been turned into a dormitory study hall. In 2000 the Minneapolis architect Leonard Parker, who was the project architect with Saarinen for Noyes, completed a meticulous renovation of the original living room with the intention to further renovate other areas of the building.

Saarinen went on to design such notable buildings as the TWA Terminal at Kennedy Airport, Dulles Airport Terminal, and the highly praised CBS Building in New York City. He died prematurely at age fifty-one, only a few years after completing Noyes. Saarinen's second wife, Aline B. Louchheim (Vassar 1935), was a well-known art critic. In an article for the *New York Times* magazine, she accurately claimed, "The son's contribution is in giving form or visual order to the industrial civilization to which he belongs, designing imaginatively and soundly within the new esthetics which the machine age demands and allows."[61]

17. Cushing House
Allen and Collens, 1927

Cushing House

Cushing House, lounge

Cushing's U-shaped plan forms an open courtyard facing Pine Walk, creating an exquisite vista of lawn and trees for its residents. Built in an "old English" style to match nearby Pratt House, Cushing resembles a manor house in its half-timber decoration, leaded windows, slate roofs, and towers. The interior is divided into two halves with each wing of the ground floor housing student rooms and the connecting section accommodating the common rooms. These included two lounges and a large dining room. Wooden paneling, traceried windows, and ornate plaster ceilings together with Jacobean-style furnishings created a medieval atmosphere in these rooms. From the back of the dining room (now lounge) extends a short wing that holds the kitchen and pantry on the ground floor. The upper floors of this wing originally housed college servants, but these rooms as well as the original student rooms on the rest of the upper floors are now used for students. Its crenellated towers, carved panels, and patterned brickwork lend Cushing a sumptuous quality, yet, in April of 1928, the college's general manager, Keene Richards, wrote to President MacCracken: "I believe this building to be as strictly utilitarian as the average factory structure, considering the purity of each, and I am sure that a careful analysis of this structure and its equipment will convince anyone that it is neither luxurious nor extravagant."[62]

Cushing was built to solve the problem of overcrowding in the college's dorms. From about 1900 until 1925, one-third of the freshman class was required to live off campus due to increasing enrollments.[63] In 1925 the trustees decided that this unsatisfactory arrangement should end despite the overcrowding that housing all students on campus would entail. All were moved onto campus with the promise that a new dormitory would be built quickly. The college felt so strongly about the situation that it actually began Cushing with borrowed money and raised funds to pay back the loan during construction. The building is named after Florence M. Cushing (Vassar 1874) in honor of her forty years of service, beginning in 1887, as one of the college's first alumnae trustees.

President MacCracken had first suggested the new dormitory be constructed as a group of buildings,

> which would resemble a village enclosure in the Old English style, using as units about 8 houses... enclosed within a brick wall.... From the point of household management such a group might contribute

materially to the Euthenics scheme, since each building could be used as a home unit for purposes of observation and experiment within the department of nutrition, hygiene and home economics.[64]

Although the need for a new dormitory had been determined independently of the euthenics program (see *Introduction*, p. 18), discussions of Cushing's design soon came to include concerns that it stand as a model of euthenics principles.[65] A letter of February 2, 1926, from college warden Jean Palmer to MacCracken supports the idea of the new dormitory stating, "Vassar is appearing as an exponent of euthenics and the present living conditions seem inconsistent (*sic*)."[66] The fundraising brochure for Cushing Hall stresses both how necessary construction is to provide on-campus housing for all students as well as the euthenics axiom "Good Health and Good Work depend upon adequate living conditions."

The final scheme did not follow MacCracken's recommendation for recreating an English village nor does it display any obvious connection with the long-forgotten euthenics curriculum apart from its provision of clearly adequate living conditions for its residents. Originally housing 130 students in 126 single and two double rooms, Cushing's cozy domesticity is a far cry from the institutional nature of collegiate residential architecture found on other college campuses.

18. Kenyon Hall

Allen & Collens, 1933; renovation, Gluckman Mayner Architects, 2002

The final piece of the euthenics group was Kenyon Gym, the third building at Vassar constructed for physical education, following the Calisthenium (later known as Avery Hall) of 1866 and Alumnae Gym of 1889.[67] It is named for the first woman president of the board of trustees, Helen Kenyon, from the class of 1905. Kenyon's design reflected ideas that were novel for their time, regarding exercise as a pleasure that should be a lifelong pursuit rather than an obligation abandoned after college. This philosophy was consistent with the euthenics curriculum's goal to provide practical preparation for life after college and to stress the importance of healthy living. At its dedication in 1934, President MacCracken noted that the building marked "the transition in physical education from its earlier function as a calisthenic drill to its incorporation as a social institution in daily life. The activities encouraged at Kenyon Hall will, for the most part, be those which young women will continue to practice after graduation."[68]

Kenyon's exterior and interior recall cozy clubhouse spaces using a design vocabulary reminiscent of late-medieval domestic architecture. The prospectus announcing the new building by college architects Allen &

Kenyon Hall

Collens related it to the idea of an English country house with farm out-
buildings, suggestive of Matthew Vassar's birthplace in Norfolk, England.[69]
Vassar's birthplace was, in fact, a far humbler structure. Kenyon Hall was
constructed out of brick with Indiana limestone trim. Using brick as the
building material provided a link with nearby Cushing House while the overall medieval revival vocabulary formed a clear connection to the rest of the
euthenics buildings constructed under MacCracken's leadership.

     The building's site, about fifty feet north of Wimpfheimer Nursery
School, continued the development of the northeast section of the campus
and gave it proximity to the playing fields, tennis courts, ice hockey rink,
and new golf course constructed on the site of recently purchased Wing
Farm. As at nearby Cushing, Blodgett, and Wimpfheimer, leaded windows,
Tudor arches, and gabled roofs create a complex exterior in which the
building is articulated as a series of distinct, individually scaled pieces. The
building's plan formed a sideways "H" with the front and rear portions
housing different types of athletic facilities connected by a corridor and
dressing rooms. In the front, the dance room, fencing room, offices, and
the swimming pool were located, while court games such as basketball,
squash, and tennis were housed in the rear. This arrangement allowed
Kenyon to be used for a variety of activities simultaneously. The indoor
swimming pool was among the nation's largest at the time of its construction. Housed in the southeastern part of the building, its exterior was punctuated by a multi-gabled roof and a series of large windows that created a
brightly-lit, well-ventilated interior.

The second story held the Body Mechanics Laboratory for the study of "correct body movements and postures" as well as a photographic and lamp room. Here the famous series of nude portraits were taken of each incoming student to evaluate her posture and to study the possible connection between body type and personality. A social room was also located on this floor, whose design recreated the atmosphere of a summer camp. A large stone fireplace, which was used during winter picnics following informal group sports activities, contributes to the rustic lodge atmosphere of this room. Throughout Kenyon's interior, cream stucco walls contrast with oak paneling and doors to continue the English manor theme of the exterior.

Despite the medieval style of the building, its athletic facilities were hailed as among the most modern of their time.[70] For some, the disparity between the building's modern function and facilities and its traditional cladding was too much. Alumna Catherine Bauer attacked the new design in an *Arts Weekly* issue of 1932, saying, "It may be one of the all-round all-American worst buildings of this generation."[71] In an argument couched in the structural honesty of high modernism, Bauer derided the design for concealing rather than revealing its true function with an exterior that suggests an arrangement of fireplaces, small cozy rooms, and multiple levels that simply does not exist. In the student newspaper, the *Miscellany News,* similar complaints were made about the proposed gym, and an alternative design featuring the striped forms and low horizontal lines of high modernism was illustrated.[72] Despite the criticism, fostered by the climate of avant-garde interest in high modernism, the construction of Allen & Collens's gracious medieval revival building went ahead as planned. It was not until the presidency of Sarah Gibson Blanding that the college embraced the architecture of high modernism, commissioning buildings by Marcel Breuer in 1951, Eero Saarinen in 1958, and Schweikher and Elting in 1959.

Walker Field House and the Athletics and Fitness Center have recently replaced Kenyon's role as the major athletic facility of the college. Kenyon is slated for renovation by Gluckman Mayner Architects. It will continue to provide space for dance instruction and rehearsal as well as squash courts in keeping with the building's original program. State-of-the-art classrooms integrating new technologies will soon be incorporated into this former gymnasium building to further enhance Vassar's teaching mission.

Mildred R. Wimpfheimer Nursery School

19. Mildred R. Wimpfheimer Nursery School

Allen & Collens, 1927

The construction of a nursery school on the Vassar campus marked a significant new development in American collegiate education. Although the nursery school was originally planned to provide child care for parents attending the Institute of Euthenics, its role quickly expanded into that of a laboratory that could provide pre-parental training for Vassar students. During the early twentieth century, ideas about children's education were undergoing rapid change. Previously, instinct had been considered sufficient for successful parenting, but this belief was replaced by the notion that parental instruction in child development is critical. The idea was that parents would benefit from observations of their children's behavior by properly trained nursery school staff while college students gained insights into childhood development by observing and working with the children at the nursery school. President MacCracken's strong interest in this new field of parental training inspired Charles Wimpfheimer to donate this building to Vassar in celebration of his daughter Mildred's graduation in 1927.

The building's site, away from the busiest parts of campus with views of the hills and fields of the Casperkill and its surrounding acres, was considered critical to the atmosphere of the nursery school.[73] This location, open on all four sides, provided the light and ventilation considered important for healthy and happy children. Its views were described in contemporary accounts as creating the "poise and quietness of spirit which are essential elements of a Nursery School atmosphere."[74] The actual teaching

Mildred R. Wimpfheimer Nursery School

at the school was organized around five areas of development tied to specific parts of the building: the cloak room for developing fine motor skills in
dressing and undressing; the toilet room for acquiring skills necessary for
personal body care; the dining room emphasizing motor control and good
eating habits; the sleeping room for developing good habits of relaxation
and sleep; and work rooms and play yard for improving motor skills and
social skills. Wimpfheimer's architecture was clearly designed with these
educational objectives in mind.

      Built of the same stone as York & Sawyer's Kendrick House of the
same year, Wimpfheimer Nursery School resembles a grand medieval
revival house set in parklike grounds on the edge of campus.[75] The building's leaded windows, gabled roofs, stone construction, and elaborately
carved trim are all in keeping with nearby Cushing, Kenyon, and Blodgett
halls. Two wings protrude at the front of the building to create a shallow terrace. The two large rooms on the main floor open directly onto the terrace,
providing an extended outdoor classroom space. The large, leaded
windows create sunny, well-ventilated spaces for classrooms. A kitchen and
dining room were also originally found on this floor.

      Upstairs, three dormers light the current kindergarten room. This
space was originally used as a sleeping room, its isolated position providing the quiet environment needed for napping children. Offices were also
housed on this floor. To the rear, the building extends to three stories due to
the slope of the site. The small classroom at the lower level opens onto the
expansive playground that wraps around the rear of the building. Originally,
this floor also held service rooms, which have now been converted to other

purposes, as well as classroom space now serving Vassar's new toddler program for two-year-olds.

Decorative features consistent with the exterior's medieval quality such as oak paneling and working fireplaces are found throughout the interior. The child-centered focus of Wimpfheimer is also apparent in its built-in cupboards, shelves, blackboards, railings, window seats, and sinks that are all constructed to the scale of the young students.

Still very much in operation as a preschool, Wimpfheimer also serves as a laboratory school. Its proximity to Blodgett Hall emphasizes its role in the child development part of the psychology curriculum while its architectural style ties Wimpfheimer visually to the entire euthenics group. Vassar's pioneering work in developing a full program in child study laid the groundwork for its later fame as a center for research into child psychology.

20. Blodgett Hall

York & Sawyer, 1928; addition, Cannon Associates, 1998

Blodgett Hall's picturesque asymmetries, gable roofs, chimneys, and leaded windows provide a visual link with the English medievalizing qualities of the other buildings originally planned for the euthenics program—nearby Cushing, Kenyon, and Wimpfheimer halls. Built of slightly rusticated gray stone, Blodgett features beautifully carved Gothic revival details both inside and out. Like Cushing, the Euthenics Building, as Blodgett Hall was once

Blodgett Hall

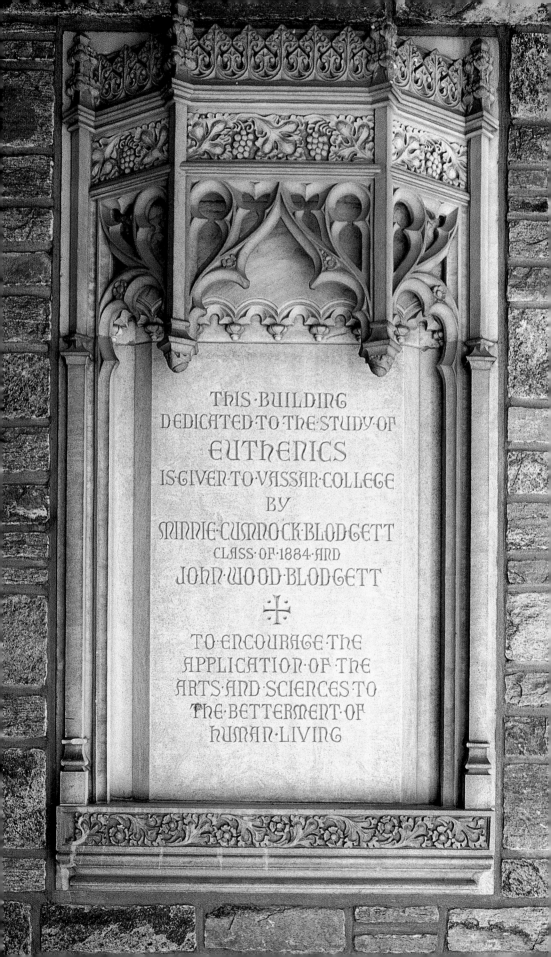

THIS·BUILDING
DEDICATED·TO·THE·STUDY·OF
EUTHENICS
IS·GIVEN·TO·VASSAR·COLLEGE
BY
MINNIE·CUMNOCK·BLODGETT
CLASS·OF·1884·AND
JOHN·WOOD·BLODGETT
✠
TO·ENCOURAGE·THE
APPLICATION·OF·THE
ARTS·AND·SCIENCES·TO
THE·BETTERMENT·OF
HUMAN·LIVING

known, forms a three-sided courtyard, in this case facing east to the Casperkill with the front of the building enjoying splendid views of Pine Walk to the west. President MacCracken himself was responsible for the siting of the building. On March 18, 1925, he wrote to architect Charles Collens asking him to correct a drawing: "The euthenics building should be turned counter-clockwise one-quarter circle, so that the open court will look directly to the east and the entrance be on the west side of the building."[76] MacCracken and other proponents of the revolutionary new curriculum were deeply concerned that the architecture of its main building be consistent with the program's objective of improving living conditions. A memo from a meeting between Henry Noble MacCracken and Professor Annie MacCleod, head of euthenics, on October 1, 1924, records, "on account of the subjects to be studied in the building it is essential that it be fully the equal in beauty of any other academic building, and that it should not depart from the higher education tradition as to architecture."[77]

In addition to classroom and laboratory space, Blodgett housed studio space for drafting and architecture classes, and a social museum. A model apartment for the study of interior design and efficient housekeeping was included on the east side of the new building, which was also intended as donor Minnie Cumnock Blodgett's residence when she visited the campus. The brochure advertising the new building and its features explains that the laboratories will be used for "the application of physics to household technology and of chemistry to problems connected with food," with the apartment serving as a laboratory for the application of art to interior decoration and design.[78] York & Sawyer's drawings identify oak wainscoting with mahogany trim and Jacobean-style plasterwork for the second-story living room. The costly detailing of the suite in the east end of the building clearly provided a luxurious prototype for its students. These expectations for a post-college life of comfort and privilege were countered by the call to service suggested by the Social Museum once found at the northwest end of the building opposite the model apartment. The museum featured exhibits on tenement housing, racism, and children's health.[79]

The inclusion of a social museum grew out of an idea initially proposed by pioneering history professor Lucy Maynard Salmon in 1917.[80] The museum served the dual purpose of providing a laboratory for training students "in techniques of handling local materials" while also hoping to become "a center of general education for the local community," as MacCracken noted in *Vassar Alumnae Magazine* in 1937.[81] In 1937, after a lengthy delay, the Social Museum opened with a loaned exhibit of photographs and models from the New York City Housing Authority entitled "The Development of Housing in New York." Reflecting the innovative and pioneering quality of the new curriculum, students were allowed to develop

OPPOSITE: *Blodgett Hall, detail*

academic work into exhibits rather than papers for some euthenics courses. These included exhibits on the dairy industry in surrounding Dutchess County with a discussion of a local milk strike and exhibits on child health activities in Dutchess County.

In 1938, ten years after the building opened, MacCracken announced that Blodgett now housed almost all courses for which it was originally intended: horticulture, food chemistry, sociological and statistical studies, economic geography, physiology, hygiene, public health, psychology, a social museum, as well as extracurricular courses in cookery and arts and crafts.[82] Despite this achievement, the euthenics program never really became a full-fledged part of the Vassar curriculum. At the opening ceremony, Mrs. Blodgett noted that "motherhood as a career for a woman is worthy of her highest gifts and that the Euthenics building served to help women in the fulfillment of that career." At the same time, in an essay published on the occasion of Blodgett's dedication, faculty member Helen Lockwood wrote: "The tradition of Vassar demands that it go out to face the bold vision of this new America. In dedicating Blodgett Hall, the College is saying that it accepts the challenge."[83] The conflict between euthenics' mixed identity as a program reinforcing women's traditional role and a groundbreaking educational movement in keeping with Vassar's tradition as a pioneer in women's education was never resolved. Many faculty members resisted participating in the euthenics curriculum and refused to move into Blodgett. Due to its low occupancy rate, part of the building was used for a student housing coop from 1933–37. After World War II, the euthenics program and the Social Museum disappeared, and Blodgett became identified as the home for social science departments such as economics, anthropology, and psychology.

In 1998 Cannon Associates made a careful addition to Blodgett below the east-facing courtyard of the main building. Housed in this addition is Blodgett's new laboratory complex, including new animal laboratories, a human perception and cognition suite, a human observation suite, and a faculty-student lounge. This elegant solution looks toward the Casperkill and takes full advantage of the picturesque landscape on its eastern facade while respecting the original integrity of the York & Sawyer design.

21. Pratt House

York & Sawyer, 1916

This spacious Tudor revival house was built for the head warden of the college. The high hedge surrounding the front garden provides a clear sense of enclosure and privacy for the only faculty house permitted on the main campus. Pratt's leaded windows and half-timbered brick construction

Pratt House

signify the beginning of a series of buildings in a late-medieval domestic style constructed under President MacCracken.

In 1913 the position of lady principal—a central figure in student life since the college's beginning—was abolished, and a board of wardens, one of whom lived in each residence house, was established. Rules governing student life were liberalized as students took increasing responsibility for their lives. Jean Palmer (Vassar 1893) was appointed head warden, a new position that warranted a new residence for the office holder. In 1914 the trustees passed a motion exempting the house for the head warden from the prohibition against constructing professors' houses on campus. The trustees approved the building on the condition that its location not interfere with the placement of future academic buildings and that it could be built without expense to the college.[84] Longtime trustee Charles M. Pratt (1896–1920) offered funding for the building, and after considerable debate, a site northeast of Alumnae Gymnasium was selected.

The size and grandeur of the house indicate the importance attached to the position of the head warden, who lived within easy reach of the wardens and students under her authority, yet separate from them. Eventually, the role of head warden was transformed into that of a modern dean of residential life. Today, Pratt House is used for meetings and as a college guesthouse.

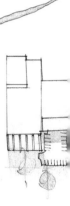

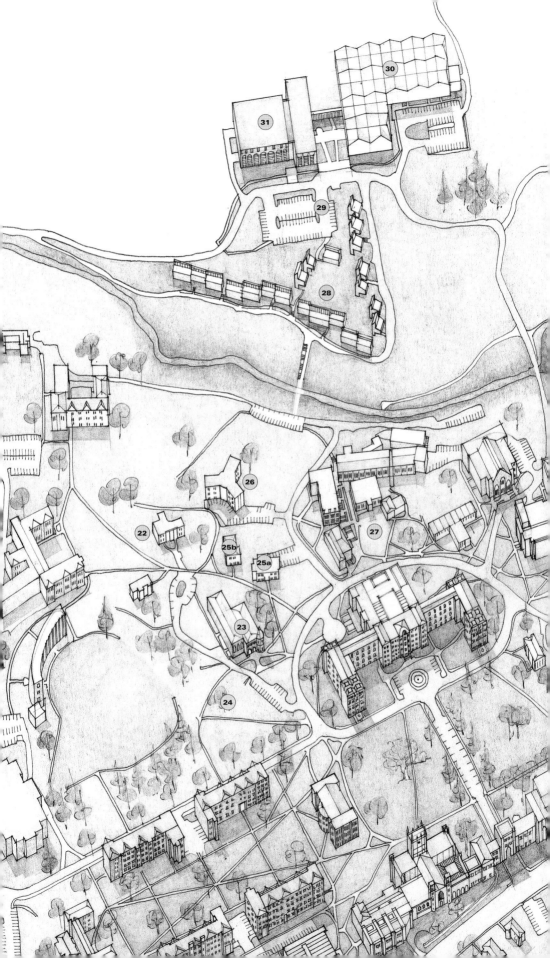

Maria Mitchell Observatory

22. Maria Mitchell Observatory

Charles S. Farrar, 1864–65; addition, 1895

Crowning a small hill approximately eight hundred feet northeast of Main stands the first of Vassar's buildings ready for use. The construction of one of the finest observatories in the nation as part of the college's original campus attests to Matthew Vassar's firm commitment to providing the best possible education at his new institution. Committed to hiring female professors, he was disappointed to find few qualified female candidates. Therefore, Vassar must have been delighted when trustee Rufus Babcock succeeded in persuading renowned astronomer Maria Mitchell to join the Vassar faculty in 1865. She was one of the two women (the other was Alida Avery) among the original eight faculty members (nine including the president).[85] Overcoming her initial reluctance to accept the position due to her own lack of advanced formal training, Mitchell ultimately moved to Poughkeepsie with her father where she would remain until her retirement shortly before her death in 1889, continuing her scientific work and inspiring her students. Upon her acceptance, the trustees undertook to provide a building with state-of-the-art facilities including not only one of the best telescopes in the country but also a nearby telegraph line linking the Vassar observatory with other observatories. Samuel F. B. Morse, one of Vassar's original trustees, was undoubtedly instrumental in bringing the modern technology of the telegraph to the college.

In its elevation and details as well as its materials, the observatory matches Main Building. Large arched windows with prominent stone keystones punctuate the upper level of the two-story brick structure. On the lower floor are segmental arched windows similar to those found on the ground floor of Main. Pairs of brick pilasters reinforce the corners of this building, too, and articulate its vertical units. Simple stone string courses mark its horizontal divisions. The building's scientific function is clearly suggested by the large dome crowning the twenty-six-foot-wide octagonal center section. Pine ribs covered by heavy sheet tin formed the original dome, which revolved using a system of sixteen cast-iron pulleys running on an iron track.[86] Three two-story wings, each measuring twenty-one by twenty-eight feet, radiate out from the octagonal center. The second floor of each wing held rooms containing specialized astronomical equipment: to the north a prime vertical room was found, to the east the transit room; a clock and chronograph room was located in the south wing, where it remains today. Charles S. Farrar, who later became Vassar's first professor of mathematics, physics, and chemistry, designed this first-rate facility for the illustrious astronomer. The observatory he planned was unique in being equipped both to support Mitchell's research and for the practical purposes of teaching.

Mitchell had attained international recognition at the age of twenty-nine for her sighting of a comet with a telescope on October 1, 1847.[87] This was the first time such an event had been recorded in the U.S. For this achievement she received a gold medal from the King of Denmark as well as other awards, and the comet was ultimately named after her. She was the first woman elected to the American Academy of Arts and Sciences in 1848, which was followed by her election to the American Association for the Advancement of Science in 1850. Mitchell continued her pioneering research in astronomy at Vassar, specializing in studies of Jupiter and Saturn as well as developing new means of recording solar activity. She remained on the faculty until 1888, the year before her death.

As a successful woman scientist and feminist, Mitchell was indeed a model for her students.[88] She was immensely successful and popular as a teacher despite the demanding level of preparation her astronomy courses required. On the first day of class, Mitchell greeted her advanced students with the remark, "We are women studying together."[89] Her influence extended beyond the realm of astronomy, as she became an active campaigner for higher education of women, inspiring her students in all of their academic pursuits. Mitchell believed that scientific study would provide her students with a way of thinking that would facilitate rationally based problem solving.[90] She also wished to broaden women's range of opportunities. An inspired teacher, Mitchell required students to conduct individual experiments and would call them from Main late at night for astronomical observations. Astronomy students also ventured further afield under her guidance; in 1869 she took a group to Iowa to observe an eclipse and in

1887, to Colorado. Mitchell's emphasis on original thinking and direct observation would become the hallmark of a Vassar education.

The observatory was also home to Mitchell and her father. Mitchell was the only professor of the college who resided outside Main, and she used her independent living quarters to host legendary gatherings known as Dome Parties.[91] These highly popular entertainments often included prominent outside guests as well as charades, poetry, and refreshments.

In recognition of her professional contributions and her advocacy for women, the observatory was designated a National Historic Landmark in 1991. At the presentation ceremony, Park Service representative Duane Pearson noted that the building was Mitchell's "home, her laboratory, and her classroom for the last 20 years of her life, and it was here that she inspired young women to think for themselves."[92] Used as the college's observatory for over a century, the building now houses administrative and classroom space. The tradition of studying astronomy at Vassar continues at the Class of 1951 Observatory, which opened in 1997.

23. Ely Hall (formerly Alumnae Gymnasium)

William Tubby, 1889; William Downing, 1906;
renovation, Olson Lewis Architects & Planners, Inc., 1994

Ely Hall

Ely Hall

The broad brick arches and squat proportions of Ely Hall lend a sturdy, muscular quality to the college's second gymnasium. The patterned brickwork, moldings, and terra cotta decorations, together with the two-story turret, recall the Romanesque revival style popularized by Henry Hobson Richardson, who used this style for collegiate buildings such as Austin Hall at Harvard. Thermal windows—semicircular openings similar to those found in Roman baths—lit the indoor swimming pool housed on the ground floor. The large exercise room (sixty-seven by forty-one feet) was also on the ground floor.[93] Its windows were originally placed high in the wall to prevent passersby from seeing those exercising within.[94] An open rafter roof and large arched windows lend an open, airy feeling to the thirty-five-foot-high space. The east wall holds a terra cotta fireplace and chimney once used to roast chestnuts and popcorn.[95] The multipurpose assembly hall on the second floor was brightly lit by large square windows along the front and sides of the building.

Ely's construction history was a troubled one. Funded by the alumnae, as its original name suggests, the donors struggled to assemble adequate resources for the modern gymnasium. Led by mathematics professor Achsah M. Ely (Vassar 1868), the alumnae raised $20,000 by 1887 for a new gymnasium, which would enable Vassar to keep pace with more recently constructed facilities at Smith and Wellesley.[96] Florence Cushing and the Boston Alumnae Club spearheaded the campaign. The ambitious program of the first design—a stone building with a visitors' gallery and running track suspended from the ceiling—proved too expensive for the available funds. The architect William Tubby, who had recently designed Pratt Gymnasium at Amherst College, substituted brick for stone and reduced the size and number of facilities in order to meet the building's budget.[97] The building did contain, however, the largest collegiate indoor swimming pool of the time, due to the generosity of trustee Frederick Thompson. Indoor tennis and basketball were played in the large second-floor hall (forty-seven by a hundred feet). Known as Philalethean Hall, this space contained a stage and was the site of the "Hall Plays" held four times a year.[98] The building provided the opportunity for Vassar to maintain its emphasis on the physical as well as the intellectual development of its students in the late nineteenth century. Each student was given a physical examination upon entrance and prescribed an individual course of exercise based on her physical condition. Three hours of exercise were required each week, one of which could be spent ice-skating during the winter.

Shortly after the formal opening of Alumnae Gymnasium in June 1890, the college began to revise its interior functions to keep up with Vassar's continuing expansion. By 1892 the second-story hall had been turned into an assembly room for day students and those forced to live off campus at the Windsor Hotel due to lack of dormitory space.[99]

In 1905 architect William Downing enlarged the building's athletic facilities by adding an extension to the back.[100] Following the construction of Kenyon Gymnasium in 1933, Alumnae Gymnasium took on other functions. Its name was changed to Ely Hall, in honor of Professor Achsah Ely, who had led the original funding campaign.[101] The most notable change during this period was the transformation, in 1937, of the exercise hall into the Aula, a space for faculty meetings.[102] President MacCracken wanted this room to emulate the halls of European universities, in some countries known as *aulas* (from the Latin word for hall), by providing a collegial setting for informal discussion and debate. Ruth Adams (Vassar 1904), the architect of several faculty houses, supervised the renovation, during which the windows were lengthened to within three feet of the floor. The room was furnished to allow for informal social gatherings as well as formal meetings and lectures. President MacCracken requested photographs of *aulas* from great universities of western Europe for the decoration of the new faculty meeting place. During this period, doctors' offices and a nurses' suite were incorporated into the building. Later, studio art moved to Ely, and the college snack bar was also briefly housed here.

In 1937 the geology department moved its offices, classrooms, and museum from the New England Building to Ely, where it remains today. The A. Scott Warthin Jr. Geological Museum is housed on the ground floor. Recent renovations to the second floor have provided enhanced office, laboratory, and classroom space for the geology and geography department. The Aula has been returned to its original beauty as its wooden floor and brick and terra cotta materials have been lovingly restored. Like many of Vassar's buildings, Ely has had many lives, which reflect the growth and evolution of the college facilities over the past century.

Outdoor Classroom

24. Outdoor Classroom
Molly S. Drysdale, 1939

The Outdoor Classroom, located near Ely Hall, was designed by Molly S. Drysdale (Vassar 1931) and donated by Russell E. Leffingwell, a trustee of the college at the time. He gave the funds to build this structure as a result of his direct involvement with the students. MacCracken noted in his book *The Hickory Limb:*

> The Trustees, on their turn, established a Committee on Undergraduate Life and discussed the general college policy quite frankly with them. It was after one of these sessions that Russell Leffingwell, formerly Assistant Secretary of the United States Treasury, and an active trustee, expressed himself as so delighted with students' maturity in dealing with these questions that he wanted to signalize the day in some way. Thus was built the open-air classroom, with its praise (by Pericles, of course) of free discussion, and of the value of action after it. For we Athenians have the peculiar honor of thinking before we act, and of acting too.[103]

Set within a grove of evergreen trees, this outdoor classroom is defined by a three-quarter circular bench that shapes the space and provides seating for fifteen to twenty people.

TOP: *Swift Hall*
BOTTOM: *Metcalf House, rear facade*

Metcalf House

25. Swift Hall and Metcalf House

Swift Hall

> *York & Sawyer, 1900; remodeled, 1941*

Metcalf House

> *York & Sawyer, 1915*

Resembling two colonial revival mansions, Swift and Metcalf represent one aspect of Vassar's tremendous growth and development under President Taylor. As the college expanded its enrollment and modernized its facilities, the infirmary and convalescent room on the fourth floor of Main were no longer sufficient for Vassar's medical needs. In 1900 York & Sawyer designed a new infirmary. Named after charter trustee Charles Swift, the new infirmary was given by Caroline Swift Atwater (Vassar 1877) in honor of her father.[104] Swift Hall's elaborate roof balustrade, columned entrance porch, dentil moldings, and central emphasis of the facade suggest a Georgian-style influence. The building's many windows provided ample light and air for the infirmary rooms housed within. Prominent stone window heads enliven its brick facade. After the completion of Baldwin Infirmary in 1940, Swift was remodeled as a classroom building and continues to serve today as the home of the history department.

Fifteen years after Swift's completion, York & Sawyer designed another building for the college's medical needs. Although more modest, the proximity and stylistic similarity of Metcalf House to Swift suggest their

Baldwin Infirmary

functional connection. Mr. and Mrs. J. H. Metcalf, parents of Cornelia Metcalf Bontecue (Vassar 1914), donated the funds for this physician's residence and convalescent home for students.[105] The physician's apartment was located on the first floor along with a laboratory for pathology and a consulting room. The latter was used for the physical examination required of freshmen. Each room for convalescing students had access to a veranda since fresh air was considered essential for their return to good health.[106] Today Metcalf houses the offices of student counseling.

26. Baldwin Infirmary

Faulkner & Kingsbury, 1940

Tucked away to the northeast of the original observatory stands Baldwin Infirmary. Conspicuous among the buildings constructed under MacCracken's presidency for its use of the modern style, Baldwin signals the end of Allen & Collens's long reign as the college's consulting architects from 1893–1937. Francis Allen had died in 1931. Six years later, Allen Collens resigned as Vassar's college architect and Waldron Faulkner of the Washington, D.C., firm of Faulkner & Kingsbury was appointed to the position.

Shortly thereafter, the college decided to replace nearby Swift Hall as the infirmary with a more modern structure and gave Faulkner's firm the commission. The four-story brick building with its flat roof lines, ample windows, and extensive use of glass blocks draws heavily from the vocabulary of modernism. Three blocklike wings extend out from a central reception area, their entranceways articulated by protruding window bays above flat-roofed porches. As one account in the *Vassar Quarterly* of December 1940 notes, President MacCracken suggested the building's shape "to minimize the number of nurses needed, to save steps and to fit the site selected."[107] MacCracken entered the project for a new infirmary with characteristic energy and concern for detail. A committee of pre-med students was formed to critique plans for the building and offer suggestions for student needs. In particular, they requested radios, facilities for studying, better lighting, and more color. Walls of glass blocks were installed at the end of corridors to brighten the interior and reduce the need for artificial lighting during the day. A sun porch as well as ample windows throughout provided maximum sun and air for recuperating patients. An isolation room, kitchen, nurses' quarters, laboratories, x-ray facilities, a minor surgery operating room, and a guest suite for parents who might need to spend the night in case of an emergency were all included in the building's program.[108]

The modern style of the building was clearly a point of discussion at the time of its construction. Captions on early photographs comment on it, and an article written by Barbara Stimson, M.D., and member of the board of trustees, begins with the question, "Why is Baldwin House built in the modern style?" Dr. Stimson suggests that the architect, Waldron Faulkner, would answer this question on scientific and aesthetic grounds whereas she offers an answer based on "how the building evolved to show that it was fitted to the needs, rather than the needs fitted to the building." Her discussion highlights the college's desire for efficiency and modernity in its medical facilities.[109]

Dr. Stimson's explanation for the building's simple forms as largely a consequence of budgetary requirements rather than aesthetic preferences suggests the modern style was adopted in a halfhearted way at Baldwin Infirmary and not embraced for its own sake. The rather utilitarian appearance of the building, which shows a modernist vocabulary but lacks the careful sense of proportioning or beautiful materials typical of more successful modernist buildings such as nearby Noyes and Ferry houses, underscores the fact of its reluctant adoption for Baldwin House. The site itself may also indicate a lack of confidence in the building's design, since it is located at the back of the main campus and screened from view by trees. Today, only the ground floor is used for an infirmary while the upper stories house administrative offices for the college.

27. Fisher Passage and Related Buildings

Fisher Passage
> *Roth and Moore Architects with Diana Balmori, 1994*

Powerhouse Theater
> *Robertson Wood Jr., 1973*

ALANA Center
> *Jeh Johnson, 1993*

Susan Stein Shiva Theater
> *Jeh Johnson, 1994*

Doubleday Studio Art Building
> *Roth and Moore Architects, 1994*

Computer Science Department and Development Offices
> *Roth and Moore Architects, 1994*

Computer Center
> *Roth and Moore Architects, 1994*

Directly behind Main lies a collection of buildings President Fergusson affectionately dubbed "Vassar's Backyard." From the beginning of the college's history, its service facilities were concentrated in this area. A steam-producing power plant, the first heating system to be located outside of the principal structure, was constructed by Houghevont Co., New York, in 1864, and was situated a safe eight hundred feet from Main. Over time other service buildings were added. In 1872 local architect James Post records the construction of the Laundry Building. The original laundry was a three-story building, thirty by forty-five feet in dimension. Its materials and style,

ABOVE: *Powerhouse Theater (left) and Susan Stein Shiva Theater (right)*
OPPOSITE: *Fisher Passage*

LEFT: *Computer Center*
RIGHT: *Doubleday Studio Art Building*

including the mansard roof, were designed to match Main Building, which stood across the carriage road. Laundry was sent from Main to this building on a tramway, then sent down a chute to the first floor for a complex series of washing, rinsing, and starching operations before moving on to the drying and sorting rooms. The third floor held facilities for fine ironing. In addition to laundry facilities, the building also housed apartments for the college engineer and other employees. West and east additions to the original laundry were constructed in 1901 and 1909, respectively. Other service structures included coal bins and workshops for carpenters, plumbers, and electricians.

The former service buildings have been converted to academic and administrative functions and are now an integral part of college life. In 1973 President Simpson began this process of readaptation with the conversion of the powerhouse into a black-box theater now know as the Powerhouse Theater. This renovation was completed by Robertson Wood, Jr.

Following this project, there was little activity in this backyard until President Fergusson launched a series of renovations in the 1990s that have reinvigorated the complex. The Fisher Passage is a beautifully landscaped walk and ramp by landscape architect Diana Balmori with Roth and Moore Architects. The passage ties this grouping of renovated industrial buildings together while also connecting it to the original campus to the west and to the Casperkill to the east. Spanning a twenty-six-foot drop in grade, the walkway is planted with cherry trees, wisteria, and other flowering plants that give color and texture to the space. This series of projects came about as a result of the recommendations originally made in the 1988 Sasaki Associates landscape master plan. Among many other suggestions, this plan called for the relocation of facilities operations to a more remote area in order to free this central space from the service functions once associated with it. Since the completion of these many renovations in the 1990s, this area has became one of the vital centers of campus life, located just east of Main Building.

In 1993 Jeh Johnson, a prominent local architect who taught architecture at Vassar (1964–2001), converted a former service building into the

TOP: *Old Laundry Building*

BOTTOM: *ALANA Center*

ALANA Center for Vassar's multicultural organizations. The following year he renovated the old coal bin and transformed it into the Susan Stein Shiva Theater. For almost forty years, Johnson taught architectural design and drafting in the tower room of Taylor's main gate to a small group of devoted students, of which 134 have gone on to professional schools in architecture. Johnson's commitment to the profession, his loyalty to the school, and his prominence in the Poughkeepsie community made him a model for the many students he mentored. Johnson also designed the original Poughkeepsie Day School, the Murphy Farmhouse apartment conversion, and nine faculty houses.

Roth and Moore Architects carefully renovated several buildings in the old industrial complex. In 1994 they transformed the former electricians and plumbers workshop into the Russell and Janet Doubleday Studio Arts Building. It houses sculpture studios on the ground floor, which open to an outdoor terrace facing the Casperkill. Extensive renovation to the brick masonry walls has produced a handsome structure that is accented by the burgundy red metal window frames throughout. The upper level, connected by a glass-block stair enclosure, includes printmaking and painting studios.

Roth and Moore Architects similarly transformed the old Service Building into the Computer Center, connecting it visually to the Doubleday Studio Arts Building by again using the burgundy red metal window frames. Accommodated here are a student computer room, open to all members of the college community, a centralized printing operation, and

Terrace Apartments

advanced laboratories as well as staff and academic offices. The college's academic and administrative computing servers are located on the floor above.

Adjacent to the Computer Center with a small walkway in between is James Post's old Laundry Building, renovated by Roth and Moore Architects in 1994, which houses the Development Office and, on the lower level, the Computer Science Department.

28. Terrace Apartments

Acorn House, Inc. with Jean Paul Carlhian of Shepley Bulfinch Richardson and Abbott, 1972

New Terrace Apartments

Sloan Architects, 2002–03

In 1970 the college, responding to the rapid increase in enrollment, had already bid the plans for a new dormitory by Hugh Stubbins, which was to span the Casperkill behind Blodgett Hall. This project gave way to more economical and expedient housing solutions: the Terrace Apartments and the Town Houses. These four- and five-person units appealed to the new coeducational student body that liked their sense of independence, an alternative to dormitory living. The first project of 50 town houses was located just west of the Vassar Lake and opened in the fall of 1971, housing 250 students. In the following year, when the college again needed more

New Terrace Apartments

housing, the administration decided to build the Terrace Apartments near the Casperkill.

The design of the Terrace Apartments coincided with the design of the new College Center by Jean Paul Carlhian, of Shepley Bulfinch Richardson and Abbott Architects. Hoping to create a more exciting design than the Town Houses, the college hired Carlhian to work with Acorn House, Inc. to adapt this well-known modular housing system into its beautiful wooded site along the Casperkill. The linear rows of apartments started along the northeastern edge of the creek, taking full advantage of the forested view to the west. They followed the line of the creek bed and then wrapped around the landscape to the south forming a courtyard configuration that established the communal center of this housing.

The inventive interior layout, with only 998 square feet per apartment, provides a sense of spatial drama that distinguishes these housing units. Beginning with the small street-level entry, the apartments are designed in a split-level configuration so that the bedrooms along the backside are offset from the living area by a half floor, affording a degree of privacy from the main double-height living room. The dramatic main space culminates in a cozy loft at the top. These four-person units have consistently provided a popular alternative to dormitory living on the campus. New Terrace Apartments have recently been completed to the east and west of the original units. These buildings invoke the vocabulary of the arts and crafts movement using wood pergolas to define outdoor communal space. The new handicap-accessible units feature a geothermal heat pump system designed to reduce the consumption of fossil fuel on campus.

29. Golf Course

1930

In 1924 Vassar purchased another 120 acres east of the main campus, on the far side of the Casperkill. In the following years, the students and faculty originated the idea of creating a golf course in this area. They funded the project by borrowing $18,000 from the college; over the next few years alumnae, faculty, and friends, led by trustee Russell E. Leffingwell, repaid the loan and created an endowment for the golf course's long-term care. The college community laid out the course themselves; Superintendent of Grounds Henry E. Downer supervised the construction, which included adding a watering system to every green for the assurance of healthy maintenance.

Early descriptions of the golf course focus not only on the layout of the course itself, but also praise the presence of wildlife around the course and its impressive views of the Hudson River Valley.

Golf Course

30. Walker Field House

Daniel F. Tully Associates, 1982; renovated, Cannon Associates, 2000

Vassar has from its inception embraced a commitment to physical education as a necessary component of a general education. In fact, the Calisthenium (Avery Hall) was the third building to be constructed in Vassar's
early history, and shortly thereafter, in 1889, the college added Ely Hall
(originally Alumnae Gymnasium), which claimed to be the first full-scale
gymnasium in a women's college. Concurrent with the opening of this facility was the establishment of the first department of physical education in
any college in the country, soon to be followed in 1895 by the founding of
the Athletic Association, marking the beginning of organized sports at
Vassar. In 1934, with the construction of Kenyon Hall, the college added new
sports programs and a state-of-the-art facility to its already developed program for young women. The opening of Walker Field House in 1982 continued Vassar's sports tradition. This 42,000-square-foot indoor sports facility
has also functioned as a gathering space for college and alumnae/i events
as it can hold up to four thousand people. Many reunions have gathered
here over the past twenty years. The Walker family, for whom the building
is named, includes several alumnae.

Designed by Daniel F. Tully Associates, the ground floor houses a
natatorium and a gymnasium now generally used for indoor tennis, volley-
ball, soccer, fencing, and baseball. The mezzanine above offers views to the
facilities below as well as dance studios and office spaces. Walker's most
distinguished feature is its peaked hyperbolic paraboloid roof structure

Walker Field House

designed to eliminate columns from the main exercise areas. This roof system was developed as an economical way to span large areas by using prefabricated wood shells supported by laminated wood beams and reinforced concrete abutments. From a distance the roof peaks are reminiscent of mountaintops.

In 2000, the college undertook a major renovation of this building, including new flooring, lighting, locker rooms, bathrooms, and training facilities, all designed by Michael Winstanley of Cannon Associates.

Athletics and Fitness Center

31. Athletics and Fitness Center

Cannon Associates, 2000

The recent addition of the Athletics and Fitness Center by Cannon Associates added another 53,000 square feet of recreational facilities, including fitness rooms and a large gymnasium with an upper-level running track. On the exterior, the center's design is characterized by its octagonal entry pavilion, large arched windows, and a one-hundred-foot-long glass corridor connecting to Walker Field House. The spacious central volume includes upper-level offices, a café, and lounge space. Its exterior, in contrast with the Walker Field House, employs a series of historical references in its expression and detailing. The center has provided another focus for student activities in the eastern section of the campus.

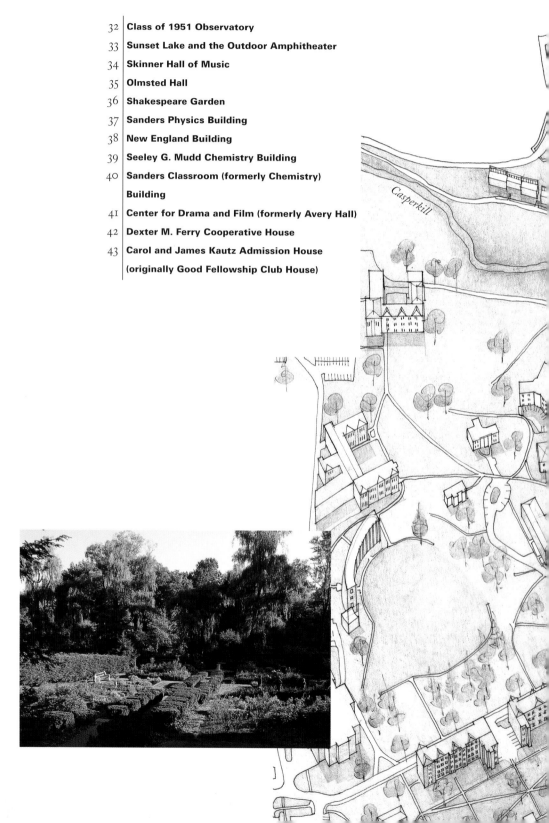

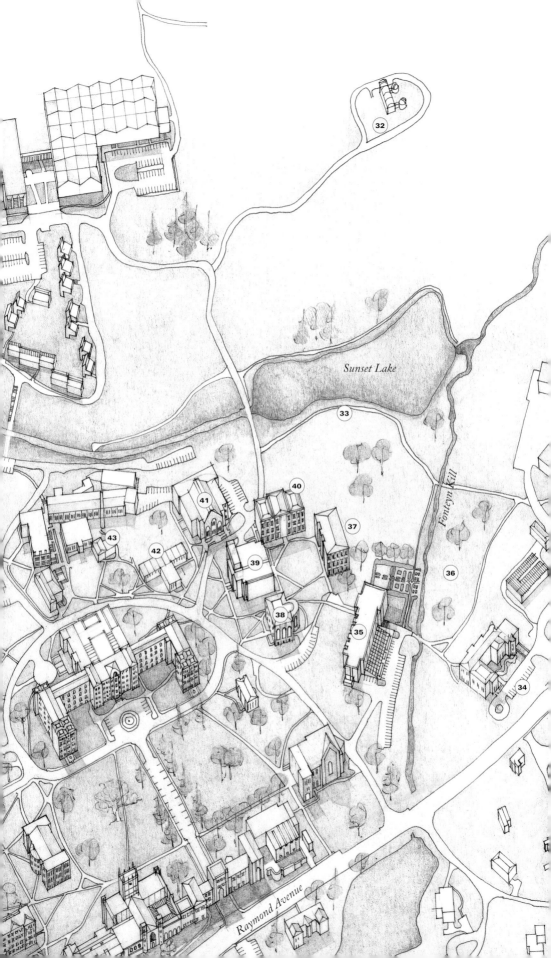

Sunset Lake

Fonteyn Kill

Raymond Avenue

32

33

40

41

43

42

39

38

37

36

35

34

Class of 1951 Observatory

32. Class of 1951 Observatory

Roth and Moore Architects, 1997

Vassar's first completed building was the old observatory located on a small knoll northeast of Main. Matthew Vassar's symbolic act of creating an eye to the great universe represented an important beginning for his emerging institution. When it was time to update the observatory, the college chose a site adjacent to the golf course, located on one of the highest elevations of the main college grounds, for the new structure. This strategic location has two advantages: it allows for unobstructed viewing of the nighttime sky with minimal light disruption and it provides one of the few direct vistas to the Hudson River Valley, just three miles to the west. From the observatory plinth the expanse of the local region can be seen as well as the sky above.

Given by the class of 1951 to mark their forty-fifth reunion, the new building was designed by Roth and Moore Architects. This thirty-year-old firm has a respectable reputation in the area of institutional and residential projects and has deployed a variety of stylistic means to accommodate different clients and sites. It is interesting to note that prior to forming his own firm in 1965, Harold Roth had been a senior designer at Eero Saarinen's office (Noyes House), working on such notable projects as the Dulles Airport and the St. Louis Arch. Although the observatory was a much more modest commission, it is a carefully designed and detailed building.

Unlike the original observatory, which was a contained object building atop a small hill, the new structure is less compact. It consists of three major volumes placed on a plinth that is oriented to the south. The entrance is on center of the linear east-west building, which is accented with a half round roof. This wing contains the classrooms and offices. The classrooms at either end have direct connections to the twenty-foot-diameter dome rooms to the south, which house thirty-two-inch and twenty-inch reflecting telescopes, equipped with CCD cameras and spectroscopes. An outdoor viewing terrace located along the central entry axis and stretching out to the south offers various positions for the portable telescopes.

The building has been intentionally designed to minimize heat pollution. In the old observatory building, the thick masonry walls retained heat from the daily sun, which was released during the evening hours directly into the surrounding atmosphere. As telescopes became more powerful and therefore more sensitive, this rising heat caused a refraction of the light from the stars that in turn created a blurred condition for viewing. It was therefore imperative to design a structure that addressed this problem. The small exterior structures are clad with a lightweight, low-thermal-mass aluminum sheathing, which helps to reflect heat away from the building. The interior spaces are well insulated to prevent heat transmission, and the dome rooms are unheated to prevent any transmission in the vicinity of the telescopes. The vaulted ceilings of the control building that contains the classrooms and offices are finished in laminated wood arches, lending warmth to these spaces through color and materiality.

33. Sunset Lake and the Outdoor Amphitheater

1915

Outdoor Amphitheater

Loring Underwood, 1915

Matthew Vassar had wanted to create a lake in the location of Sunset Lake, but he died too soon to realize his idea. It was MacCracken who began his presidency with this popular addition—made by damming the Fonteyn Kill—to the campus and soon afterwards developed an outdoor amphitheater, located on the west side of the lake, which replaced an earlier version located at the top of Sunset Hill. Vassar's resident landscape architect, Loring Underwood, exploited the topography of the hill and natural plantings to design this theater space. Canadian hemlocks and Norway spruces form the backdrop to the theater with Sunset Lake in the distance. A row of Japanese yews bordering a constructed gully separates the stage from the audience. Aside from serving as a space for all kinds of performances, the theater's most important ceremony since the 1960s has been graduation, when up to four thousand people gather to celebrate this event.

The area around Sunset Lake and the amphitheater has been planted many times with different sets of flowering, fruit, and ornamental

TOP: *Outdoor Amphitheater*
BOTTOM: *Sunset Lake*

trees. In 1926 flowering crabapple trees were planted on the lower slopes of the lake to replace the old apple orchard that had once grown here, and a Vassar mother donated the funds to plant the daffodils on the east side of the lake. One of the area's most notable transformations took place when Franklin Delano Roosevelt, a trustee of the college from 1923 until his death in 1945, urged the planting of the great pines along Sunset Lake as a practical demonstration of the principle of reforestation. When, in 1969, the aesthetic integrity of Sunset Lake was put in jeopardy by plans to build Vice President Duggan's residence on its slope, it was the Vassar students who protested and saved the area from development. That fall, frustrated that their pleas had not been heard, students vandalized the foundations of the construction, and the college decided to move the house to another site. Sunset Lake remains in its idyllic condition for future generations to enjoy.

34. Skinner Hall of Music

Charles Collens, 1932

Skinner Hall of Music, one of Vassar's most beautiful buildings, is reached by crossing a small footbridge over the Fonteyn Kill. Nestled into a hillside, its idyllic, slightly remote setting emphasizes its fairytale-castle appearance. Named for Belle Skinner (Vassar 1887), its medieval style was regarded as appropriate partly due to Skinner Hall's location near two other buildings of medieval style: the chapel and Taylor Hall. President MacCracken described

Skinner Hall of Music

Skinner as "although medieval in character...entirely practical and with no waste space."[110]

A building specifically for music had long been in the planning. By 1904 President Taylor had declared that the hill behind the chapel, then known as Barn Hill, should be developed for a music building. His early scheme included a picturesque bridge across the ravine. During Taylor's tenure, the barns were removed, and the ravine began to be prepared for a building. Originally, trustee Dr. Henry Sanders had planned to give a building for art and music, but when the Pratts donated money for the art building, Sanders was persuaded by Taylor to bequeath money for the chemistry building instead.[111]

Skinner Hall, weather vane

Skinner's leaded window panes, gray fieldstone walls, spire, slate roof, and turret are reminiscent of collegiate Gothic buildings found elsewhere at Vassar as well as across other contemporary American campuses. Here, however, the medievalizing style is directly tied to the interests of the building's namesake. Belle Skinner spent the years from 1881 to 1883 in Vassar's preparatory department before going on to the college program and receiving her degree in 1887. Throughout her college career and afterwards, collecting music and musical instruments was her first love. She aided many musicians in their careers but this was only one of many causes she supported during her lifetime.[112] Skinner also established a fellowship that enabled Vassar graduates to study history in French provincial universities. In addition, she wrote about the destruction of France during World War I in *Atlantic Monthly, Review of Reviews*, and the *Outlook,* and participated actively in the postwar restoration of ruined French villages. She was awarded several honors by the French government, including the *Medaille de la Reconnaissance Francais*, particularly for her work toward the rebuilding of the village of Hattonchatel, located south of Verdun. She gave $1,000,000 toward its reconstruction.[113] Skinner Hall was given, with an

OPPOSITE: *Skinner Hall, Mary Anna Fox Martel Recital Hall*

Skinner Hall, detail

endowment, by her brother, William Skinner, in honor of her memory. It acknowledges both her love of music and French culture.

Skinner Hall's interior spatial arrangements were carefully planned by Professor George Sherman Dickinson of the music department with practical considerations in mind.[114] Dickinson also designed Skinner's weather vane, which forms the initials of George Coleman Gow in its musical notations. Gow was a professor of music from 1895–1932, who continued to promote music as a subject of serious study. Music became a regular, rather than special, department in 1891 as Vassar led the way in developing a true music curriculum.

Skinner consists of three sections, each of which contains rooms for particular aspects of music education. Classrooms for theory and history, the library, offices, and studios are found in the central part of the building. On the first floor of the central section are the department offices and a reception room originally furnished by Miss Skinner's class (1887).[115] The library's two-story reading room has a beamed ceiling and medieval-style light fixtures. Pointed arch openings screen this room from the adjacent open stacks. The reading room extends into the polygonal turret, a feature that contributes heavily to the medieval character of the exterior. A small museum for Vassar's collection of musical instruments is housed in a beautiful medieval setting above the library.

The library, offices, and classrooms of the building's central section are separated from the recital hall and practice rooms by a ring of corridors that act as sound barriers. The practice rooms are located to the south and west of the library. Opposite, in the north wing of the building, is the recital hall. It was placed there to take advantage of the natural slope of the site in the construction of its floor. Its airy interior accommodates five hundred people, with a medieval vaulted ceiling rising two-and-a-half stories above the floor. The recital hall, with its stage and adjacent rooms, was planned for various functions; it serves as a hall for small concerts and recitals, a large lecture hall for classes, and a place for dramatic presentations with music. The performance space can be modified in a variety of ways: part of the audience floor can be lowered to open an orchestra pit, footlights can be installed, and scenery lowered into

Olmsted Hall

position. A replica baroque organ, built by Paul Fritts in 2002, is also housed in the recently renovated recital hall, now called the Mary Anna Fox Martel Recital Hall.

A smaller recital space, which seats about one hundred people, is located upstairs from the recital hall. Known as Thekla Hall, this smaller space with a fireplace at one end and a platform surmounted by a rose window opposite it, provides a setting for rehearsals as well as entertainment by the department.

35. Olmsted Hall

Sherwood, Mills and Smith, 1972

With the construction of Olmsted Hall, gift of the Olmsted family, the biology department was contained in one building for the first time in years. This state-of-the-art facility was considered one of the best-equipped science buildings at an undergraduate institution of its era. Its placement between the science quad and Skinner Hall, however, was very controversial at the time of planning. The view from the quad looking southwest over the Shakespeare Garden to Skinner had been one of the most cherished vistas at the college, and the insertion of this 72,000-square-foot building raised plenty of eyebrows. In response to the inevitable destruction of this walk, the architects, Sherwood, Mills and Smith, created a new passageway through the building by inserting a large opening into it, thus maintaining some visual continuity between the quad and Skinner. The view to Skinner unfolds as one walks through Olmsted's lower level, which is carefully integrated into the side of the hill, creating a strong edge to the Fonteyn Kill.

Sherwood, Mills and Smith built many institutional buildings, including the Wilson Quad at Princeton. The firm's expertise lay in its programmatic and functional capabilities rather than original space-making or aesthetic characteristics. The building's late-modernist expression is representative of the 1970s period in American architecture. It is derived from the earlier "brutalist period," which originated in England in the 1960s and preferred a functional expression above any decorative or aesthetically driven ideas.

Olmsted is a brick-clad concrete building that follows a tripartite linear organization with an interior atrium space located between two adjacent wings of unequal length. The planning of the programmatic spaces is clear and easily understood. The wing to the southwest contains three levels of offices, research laboratories, and classrooms while the northeast wing contains lecture halls and the library. The main atrium space, directly off the entrance, is elevated one half-level above the ground plane. Access to its upper level is gained by an open stairway, which owing to its heavy expression, has the effect of dissecting the space rather than unifying it. A skylight of less than pure geometric proportions covers the space. The interior materials of the laboratory floors are cinderblock walls, concrete floors, and exposed ductwork, all of which are consistent with its exterior functionalist expression. In other areas, such as the library, interior finishes are of a higher quality. Though one might argue that this building lacks the kind of sophistication and thoughtful detailing that occurred in the previous generation of buildings on campus, Olmsted is a good example of the 1970s period in architecture and has functioned well as a home for the biology department.

36. Shakespeare Garden

1916

Winifred Smith of the English department and Emmeline Moore of the botany department initiated the idea of this garden as part of the tercentenary of Shakespeare's death. There are many Shakespeare gardens around the world, but what distinguished this one was the fact that the two classes of Smith and Moore designed and built it themselves. Using many of the species of plants mentioned in Shakespeare's writing, the students obtained the seeds from Stratford-upon-Avon.

The garden had to be rebuilt after the construction of Olmsted Hall and was later remodeled along the lines of an English flower and herb

Shakespeare Garden

garden. It has been substantially renovated during the past fifteen years. The recently installed sculptures were originally brought from Italy by Matthew Vassar.

37. Sanders Physics Building

Ewing and Allen, 1926

Sanders Physics Building completed the science quadrangle formed by its companion building, Sanders Classroom (formerly Chemistry Building), New England Building, and Vassar Brothers Laboratory (formerly on the site of the current Mudd Chemistry Building).

      The construction of Sanders Physics Building continued the modernization and enlargement of the facilities available in Vassar Brothers Laboratory begun with the construction of the Sanders Classroom Building in 1909. Dr. Henry Sanders, trustee of the college, bequeathed $150,000 to Vassar in his will for a physics laboratory in honor of himself.

      In contrast to the medieval revival forms that dominate much of the rest of the campus buildings from this period, Ewing and Allen used a strictly neoclassical vocabulary here in keeping with the adjacent New England and Sanders Classroom buildings. The elevation of Sanders Physics is organized in a gridlike composition as brick pilasters with limestone capitals divide the facade into a series of bays. The windows of the two major floors are separated by wide bands of brick that create a

Sanders Physics Building

horizontal emphasis between the vertical axis of the pilasters running from the roof down between the half windows of the basement level. As at New England Building, a heavy classicizing cornice crowns the structure. The ends of the building project slightly to break up the flat facade and frame its central space, which contains the two primary volumes of the interior: a lovely wood-paneled library located slightly below the first-floor level with a major lecture room above.

Sanders Physics is the home of the physics and astronomy department. Implementation of the Ellenzweig Associates classroom master plan will provide for a substantial renovation to improve facilities and update technologies in classrooms and labs.[116]

38. New England Building

York & Sawyer 1901; addition, 1919;
renovation, Liscum McCormack VanVoorhis, 2001

Above the doorway of the New England Building protrudes a piece of Plymouth Rock, significant for the building's identity in two ways. As the name of the building suggests, New England was the gift of alumnae living in the New England area, who were tireless in their efforts to upgrade the facilities of their alma mater.[117] Many of them had also been responsible for the construction of Alumnae Gymnasium (Ely Hall) in 1889. Florence Cushing, one of the leaders in the fundraising effort and one of the three

New England Building, front door

alumnae trustees first elected to the board in 1886, had traveled to Plymouth after learning that part of the famous rock had accidentally broken off, to secure a piece for the new building.[118]

The incorporation of this relic also suggests the building's original function: New England was built to house the natural sciences of biology, physiology, mineralogy, and geology. Its position on the south side of Main continued the development of this side of the campus as a center for the sciences, begun by the construction of Vassar Brothers Laboratory for the study of chemistry and physics in 1880. The first entirely new building to be constructed since the college's opening, Vassar Brothers Laboratory stood on the current site of Mudd Chemistry Building until its demolition in 1938. Its steeply pitched gable roofs, corner pilasters, arched windows, and brick construction tied the laboratory visually to Main Building. New England Building, although also of brick, employs an entirely different style. The

New England Building

large windows, typical of science buildings of the time, provided ample light for using the microscopes with natural rather than artificial light although the building was wired from the beginning in anticipation of electricity coming to the campus.[119]

The building's window forms, ornate ironwork, and prominent neoclassical decoration are typical of beaux arts–style academic buildings found at this time at many American campuses such as Columbia University. The two-story brick building is crowned by a heavy classical cornice of Bedford stone. An ironwork classical garland that projects upwards from its edge animates the roof above. The facade is articulated as an alternation of voids and solids. Prominent two-story pilasters crowned with limestone capitals divide the front facade into five bays. Large two-story windows subdivided by green mullions and ornate railings occupy each bay. The limestone capitals of the pilasters continue around the top of the windows as ornamental trim. Each window arch has an elaborate volute marking the position of the keystone. The overall plan of New England, a rectangle with a protruding apse to the rear housing a lecture hall, is a smaller-scale version of York & Sawyer's first classroom building at Vassar, Rockefeller Hall of 1897.

Inside, a central hallway divides the ground floor in half and contains a dramatic staircase leading up to the second floor. The large semicircular lecture room holds 120 seats and is found at the rear of the main stairway. The left side of the ground floor held the mineralogy laboratory, geology office, and geology lecture room. On the right were rooms for botany and zoology. Upstairs a large laboratory ran across the front of the building with a small lecture room to the left of the stairs and the library to the right.[120] A row of museum cases along the large central hallway displayed selected items from the college's large natural history collection, which was principally housed in Avery Hall at this date.[121] The basement held rooms with equipment for scientific research and experimentation.

Currently the building holds a wide variety of multidisciplinary programs. A recent renovation to the building provided new offices and a seminar room on the third floor.

39. Seeley G. Mudd Chemistry Building

Perry Dean Rogers & Partners, 1984

The Seeley Greenleaf Mudd Fund, whose name conveys the original energy-saving spirit of this building, provided the major grant to fund a new chemistry building for Vassar. Early in her presidency, Virginia Smith and the board hired engineer Fred Dubin of Dubin-Bloome Associates to develop a new type of science facility that would deploy state-of-the-art

Seeley G. Mudd Chemistry Building

sustainable design principles. As the planning proceeded, however, the college recognized the need to hire an architect to collaborate with the engineers in order to properly program and design the space. Perry Dean Rogers & Partners developed and completed the design, and the building that stands today bears its mark. This architectural firm is one of Boston's oldest practices, known for its early work in the area of restoration, most notably that of Colonial Williamsburg in the 1930s. More recently, the firm has established a credible reputation in educational and institutional work around the country, using the basic palette of materials that we see on the Seeley Mudd Building.

The building sits on the site of the former Vassar Brothers Laboratory, which was torn down in the 1930s, leaving the site open until the construction of Mudd. Dubin had originally sited the new structure on the south side of the Sanders Physics Building to take advantage of the southern exposure; however, Dubin was unable to create a workable plan, and college officials expressed concern about its proximity to the beloved Shakespeare Garden. Perry Dean Rogers & Partners successfully proposed the current location, which completes the science quad enclosure, while taking advantage of a southern exposure.

The massing of the three-story building is skillfully articulated by a series of brick and limestone walls that enclose volumes of glass block. This configuration has a postmodern expression characteristic of this period. Its basic planning and expression are derived from classical architectural models, but here those strategies are mixed with contemporary materials. The brick volume on the north is scaled to match the neighboring science quad buildings. Its facade is delineated by a series of horizontal bands of inset brick. These reduce the visual impact of this mass and serve as a reference to the brick detailing of the adjacent New England Building. The southern all-glass facade is punctuated by the glass-block entrance volume that is inserted into this modified Trombe wall. The energy-efficient double wall includes an exterior portion made of steel-framed plate glass suspended two feet beyond the inner brick wall. Sunlight-heated air circulates up the side of the wall through the building's internal mechanical system to heat and ventilate the interior. Windows on the interior and exterior of the double wall are aligned to frame views. The copper cladding of the upper volume pays homage to the roof materials of its neighbors and conceals the hefty mechanical equipment located on the roof, including the solar

TOP: *From left, Sanders Physics Building, Mudd Chemistry Building, Sanders Classroom Building, and Center for Drama and Film*
BOTTOM: *Sanders Classroom Building*

collectors of the building's heated water supply. The vertical missile-shaped sculptures on the roof vent the interior central air duct system. The interplay between the limestone base, the brick walls, the glass block volumes, and the spirited roofscape lends this building a dynamic quality suggestive of its internal program. Unfortunately, its energy-saving features have never met their promised performance. The complex system never worked to the full extent of its architects' design intentions and was very labor-intensive to operate. Several elements were eventually modified or shut down.

The logic of the exterior articulation of volumes does not carry through to the internal planning of this 42,000-square-foot interior. The strong symmetrical volumetric entries on the north and south, for example, suggest a public main hall connecting the two and creating a formalized entrance to the entire science quad. Instead, the laboratories are located in this central position. This, along with the split-level entry sequence, some-what compromises the circulation on the main floor.

The interior surfaces, finishes, and exposed structure and mechanical systems express the building's program. The laboratories are equipped with task-ambient fluorescent light sources, another energy-saving feature that locates the light directly over the working surfaces, thus providing an efficient and cost-effective lighting system. The exposure of the mechanical ducts allows for easy and accessible maintenance. In spite of some of its drawbacks, one must admire the ambitions of this building as the home for the chemistry department and as an exemplary step towards more energy-conscious architecture.

40. Sanders Classroom (formerly Chemistry) Building

Ewing & Chappelle, 1909;
renovations, Hutchins, Evans and Lefferts Architects, 1988–89

Sanders Classroom Building was donated to update and enlarge the college's science facilities by trustee Dr. Henry Sanders in honor of his wife, Eleanor Butler Sanders, a progressive woman active in New York public life.[122] From its beginning, Vassar emphasized science as an important part of its curriculum. It was the first women's college to have a separate building designed for laboratory use—Vassar Brothers Laboratory built in 1880 and torn down in 1938.[123] The original faculty counted four science specialists among its six professors, in keeping with Matthew Vassar's dream to create a women's college commensurate with the well-known male institutions. The Vassar science curriculum taught physical science through experimentation, following the model of Yale University. Fifteen years after the college's opening, President Caldwell urged the trustees to construct larger and safer facilities for the science program. The rooms on the first floor of Main designated for chemistry and science classes did not have proper ventilation and there was a constant risk of explosion. The construction of Vassar Brothers Laboratory and later the Sanders Classroom Building provided relief.

The neoclassical vocabulary and materials of Sanders Classroom Building match those of the adjacent Physics Building with a similar use of pilasters and string course to articulate its central facade. At Sanders Classroom, however, the central portion of the building is further emphasized as it projects beyond the wings to either side. The roof of the central section is raised by a half story with large skylights illuminating the top story. The core of the interior, as at the Physics Building, is formed by a large lecture hall, which will be upgraded as part of the new classroom master plan. Sanders Chemistry Building underwent a major renovation that modernized its interior and provided additional classroom space. It is now the home of the English and classics departments and the Asian studies program.

41. Center for Drama and Film (formerly Avery Hall)

Avery Hall

J. A. Wood, 1866

Center for Drama and Film

Cesar Pelli & Associates, 2003

The Center for Drama and Film, designed by Cesar Pelli & Associates, is built on the site of the historic Avery Hall, a nineteenth-century brick structure that was the third building to rise on the Vassar campus. Avery Hall's many name changes, which include the Museum Building, Assembly Hall, and Avery, the name it received in 1931 in honor of Alida C. Avery, the first resident physician and professor of hygiene and physiology at Vassar from 1865 to 1874, suggest the building's many functions throughout the college's history. Originally known as the Gym, it was principally built as a riding school and calisthenium.[124] Although it matched both Main and the observatory in its colors and material, it was quite different stylistically. In contrast to Renwick's Second Empire–style building, architect J. A. Wood used the popular Lombard Romanesque style. The building's brick surface was enriched with a series of corbel tables under the cornices and hood moldings that framed the window surrounds. The two square towers flanking the building were once, and are now again, topped with mansard roof forms similar to those found in Main, and the polygonal turrets framing the facade had distinctive conelike tops.

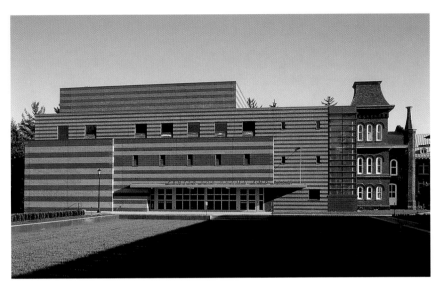

Center for Drama and Film

The original Calisthenium occupied a thirty-by-eighty-foot hall on the north side of the building.[125] It was provided with equipment that enabled students to follow a program of exercise prescribed by Dr. Dio Lewis, a well-known figure of the time who pioneered the development of physical education for everyone.[126] Students were obliged to exercise two to four times per day in half-hour blocks. A more specialized program was devised for those with identified "deficiencies." The indoor riding ring was in the central part of the building. Stalls for twenty-three horses, carriage rooms, carpenters and joiners shops as well as employee housing were located in the basement. The building also held a bowling alley, music practice rooms, and a concert stage and hall.

Financially, the riding school was not a success and despite students' protests, the college decided to close it in 1873. Thus began the first of a long series of revisions to the building as its function changed. After a $27,000 renovation, the Calisthenium reopened in 1875, renamed the Museum.[127] The art gallery moved from the fourth floor of Main into the former riding ring, and the college's Museum of Natural History also expanded from its cramped quarters in Main to a space in the front of the old Riding Academy.

In 1918 the former Museum Building was renamed Assembly Hall as its stage became the site of dramatic productions following the destruction of Main's rear wing in the fire of 1918. The completion of Skinner Hall in 1932 led to another change. As the music department moved to new quarters, the classics and English departments arrived from Rockefeller Hall.[128] Drama became an independent department in 1937 and established its headquarters there.

Center for Drama and Film

The English, classics, and Asian studies departments have recently moved to Sanders Classroom Building, bringing to an end the riding school's long history of accommodating Vassar's diverse needs.

*Built without a foundation, Avery Hall had so many structural issues at the advanced age of 135 years that it made more sense to take it down and rebuild than to attempt yet another renovation. As its facade is so full of character and Avery holds such an important place in the hearts of many alumnae/i, the decision was made, however, to retain the facade and incorporate it into the design of the new Center for Drama and Film. The preservation of the facade was funded by the Class of 1953.

Built on the footprint of the old building, the new center is in deliberate contrast to the historic facade. The two glass-enclosed stairways that flank the facade create a transition to the new building, clearly marking the 140-year gap in their construction. The forms of the new center are simple interlocking masses, defined in stripes of dark gray, light gray, and red masonry blocks. The width and density of the gray stripes vary to accentuate the play of forms. The window frames are burnt orange, and the canopy above the student entrance is painted in bright orange. The building's striped pattern, its intense colors, and simple forms give it an exciting character while the composition is elegant and serene.

The creative tension between the old and the new is philosophically appropriate for a Center for Drama and Film. As Cesar Pelli said in an interview during the early stages of the project:

> The relationship of the old and the new reflects very clearly the state of the performing arts today. While there is still a very strong theater tradition, from Shakespeare to the present day, there is also a great deal of experimentation and new developments in film and video. . . . In the character of what's happening in these artistic and intellectual and academic disciplines, there is this tension, which is actually life-giving and sustaining, between the old and the new.[129]

At the heart of the new building is a 330-seat theater suitable for dramatic performances, rehearsals, lectures, and film and video presentations. The theater has been designed as a laboratory and an efficient teaching facility, but is also a handsome, state-of-the-art professional theater. New facilities for the drama department include scene, prop, and costume shops; a dressing room; and a theatrical design lab. New facilities for the film department include a 110-seat film screening room; a cutting-edge film studio and multimedia laboratory; three editing suites; offices for computer support; and a second, smaller screening room.

Pelli's Center for Drama and Film brings together disparate elements and objectives. The mass of the new building balances the old facade of Avery Hall. At the same time, its contemporary character creates a clear tie with Marcel Breuer's neighboring Ferry House. The Frances Daly Fergusson Quadrangle, the elegant, minimalist courtyard defined by the two buildings and connecting to the nearby Powerhouse Theater, was designed by Diana Balmori and is envisioned as an important gathering space.

*The text on the new Center for Drama and Film was written by Julia Van Develder, Vassar College

42. Dexter M. Ferry Cooperative House

Marcel Breuer, 1951; original landscape design realized, 1997;
exterior and interior restoration and renovation, Herbert Beckhard Frank Richlan
& Associates, 2001–02

The opening of Ferry House must have caused quite a stir due to its architectural style. As Sarah Blanding's first building project, this modest yet ambitious structure introduced the Vassar community to the realm of contemporary architecture and challenged the prevailing notions of academic domesticity.

Designed in the late 1940s, Ferry House employed the architectural vocabulary and spatial planning concepts of the European International Style as interpreted by the Bauhaus-trained Hungarian-born designer Marcel Breuer (1902–81). Breuer studied at the Weimar Bauhaus and later, in 1925, returned to the Bauhaus now located in Dessau to become master of the woodworking shop under the direction of Martin Gropius. After Hitler closed the Bauhaus, Breuer moved to the United States to teach at Harvard's Graduate School of Design where Gropius had become the dean. The two also formed a private partnership until 1941 when Breuer established his own office and moved to New York City. In 1949 he prominently displayed his Exhibition House in the courtyard of the Museum of Modern Art in New York, thus securing his position as a major figure in the development of the International Style in America. After the Ferry House

Dexter M. Ferry House

Dexter M. Ferry House, interior

commission, Breuer began to design larger institutional buildings including such notables as the Whitney Museum in New York City, the UNESCO Headquarters in Paris, and the IBM Research Center in New York.

Ferry House, designed to take visual advantage of Vassar's beautiful landscape, has always seemed slightly out of place in its location behind Main Building. In fact, the building, which was to provide additional dormitory space, had originally been planned for a site between Strong House and the Students' Building; however the board agreed to find a less visible site after having received so many objections to its avant-garde appearance.

The building's donor, Dexter M. Ferry, had already commissioned Breuer to design a modern addition to his Georgian-style home in Baltimore; it was his daughter Edith (Vassar 1932), however, who suggested that Breuer also be the architect of the communal residence of Ferry House. She later commissioned him to design her well-known Hooper House in 1960. The Ferry family had already been very generous donors to Vassar: Blanche Ferry Hooker (Vassar 1899) and Queene Ferry Coonley (Vassar 1896), sisters of Dexter, were the donors of Alumnae House.

Ferry House was managed as a cooperative living arrangement in which students themselves performed the domestic duties associated with college life, an arrangement that had been a part of Vassar's history since the 1930s. The earliest coop was located in Raymond House and then Blodgett, home of the euthenics program, before it was moved to the Wing Farm House (Palmer House) in 1938. The war disrupted the cooperative tradition and had left the college with shortages of both dorm space as well as domestic employees. Therefore, Blanding moved quickly to bring this project to realization.

The building's late-International style, coupled with the regional influences that mark the American transformation of this movement, has secured its place in the history of American architecture. The inclusion of white-painted brick, wood infill panels, and flagstone floors—incorporating the novel use of radiant heat throughout the floor slab—represents a characteristic palette of materials of this time. The building successfully incorporates a domestic quality within the vocabulary of a modern sensibility. As opposed to his "Long House" type, Breuer called this configuration a "binuclear" arrangement in which public and private activities are formally separated by volume and spatial composition. In Ferry House the ground floor is designed as a series of flexible spaces that may be rearranged by sliding doors and panels depending on their function. The kitchen at the front of the volume is separated behind a sliding horizontal window that overlooks the public rooms of dining, living, and study areas. The faculty apartment (now student housing) is located at the far end of this floor in the most secluded portion of the plan. The exterior walls of these ground-floor public spaces are made of floor-to-ceiling glass with sliding doors, which, when open, bring the landscape inside, thus expanding the modest dimensions of the house. The lower volume engages the landscape through the use of a continuous series of low walls that merge the gardens with the building. With its minimal dimensions, the lower floor forms an elegant base to the rotated raised bedroom wing, allowing a large portion of the ground plane to remain open to the surrounding campus.

The upper level, "floating" among the treetops, houses dorm rooms for twenty-six students. Constructed of steel resting on brick piers, this wing is oriented east-west so that both sides of rooms receive direct sunlight during the day. A pipe-supported tensile-cable sunscreen system protects the western facade and creates another layer of privacy on the building's public front. The screen, fabricated in individual sections, allows thin strips of light to engage the facade and creates a dynamic quality of sunlight throughout the day. The volumetric privacy of these upper rooms is further accentuated by the position of the adjacent roof garden over the lower-level public rooms.

Breuer himself worked intensely on this project, designing much of the internal bedroom cabinetry himself. The double rooms include built-in furniture for desks and closets, which create a well-designed separation of sleep and study spaces for the roommates. He was involved in all of the detailing including the selection of furniture by Saarinen, Thonet, and Eames, and of interior fabrics from Knoll Associates. The progressive nature of the design is matched by Breuer's socially progressive office structure.

During the design of Ferry House, Breuer had only five employees in his office, of which two were women, Belva Barnes and Beverly Green, an African-American.

At Breuer's dedication speech in October 1951, he read a poem he had written for the occasion:

> Often you ask: where and how and what are AESTHETICS,
> beyond functions needed?
> Colors which you can hear with ears;
> Sounds to see with eyes;
> The void you touch with your elbow;
> The taste of space on your tongue;
> The fragrance of dimensions;
> The juice of stone.[130]

In 1997 the original landscape design was realized through a gift from Patricia Parton Rosenwald (Vassar 1956). In 2001 the college consulted with Herbert Beckhard to oversee the renovation of the building. Beckhard had joined the Breuer firm in 1952 and later became a partner in the firm of Marcel Breuer and Herbert Beckhard Architects, which lasted until Breuer's death in 1981.

43. Carol and James Kautz Admission House (originally Good Fellowship Club House)

Pilcher & Tachau 1908; renovations, Linda Yowell, 1995

Carol and James Kautz Admission House

Kautz Admission House is an arts and crafts–style stucco building with a deep veranda and projecting eaves exhibiting the boxy low profile characteristic of its style. The charming interior retains many of its original details including a tiled fireplace and finely carved wooden moldings. The house was designed by the firm Pilcher & Tachau (architects of Jewett House) as a social club for the employees and opened in March 1908. Lewis Pilcher was a professor of art at the college from 1900–11 and later became the New York State Architect and dean of architecture at Pennsylvania State College. For many years, this building was underutilized and obscured by overgrown shrubbery. Under President Fergusson, the Admission House was recovered and restored to its original beauty. Renovated by architect Linda Yowell (Vassar 1973) with funds donated by Chair Emeritus of the board of trustees James Kautz and his wife, Carol (Vassar 1955), the building now provides an elegant setting for the Admissions Office. The original living room, now the reception area for admissions, is furnished with arts and crafts–style furniture complementary to the building's vocabulary.

The building's earlier function as a social club for the employees reflects Vassar's history as a socially minded institution. The idea of a club for college workers dates back to 1890, when an organization known as the Steadfast Club was formed, which lasted for approximately one year.[131] Membership was open to all college maids, faculty, and students, with the aim of offering college servants, as these employees were then called, educational opportunities such as instruction in arithmetic, penmanship, and English. Over the next few years, students occasionally organized events for the maids and attempted to establish a library and parlor for them. After 1898 the Christian Association held regular social and devotional meetings for the college employees. In 1901 the Vassar Chapter of the College Settlements Association developed the idea of a clubhouse. Following approval by the Students' Association and the trustees in 1902, students, faculty, and alumnae donated $36,000 over the next seven years for the construction and endowment for this facility.[132]

The club welcomed all maids as members, and in an effort to encourage self-governance, officers of the club came from the members rather than the student body. A trained social worker was hired to live in the house and act as supervisor while a student committee acted as financial overseers and activity directors.[133]

The clubhouse provided a setting for a range of activities, both recreational and educational. The living room, furnished with a piano and Victrola, provided a place where the maids could relax and entertain guests. Adjacent to this was a small dining room. A circulating library for club members was located off the living room. A fully-equipped laundry and kitchen were built in the basement; the latter was used for cooking classes and preparation for private entertaining. The top floor housed a sewing room, enabling members to make their own clothes; a convalescing room;

Admission House, interior

and the sitting room for the resident supervisor. A range of classes was offered in subjects such as English, drawing, music, and botany. Members could also hold parties in the clubhouse, and on specified nights, it was used for entertaining male guests in a chaperoned setting.[134] The lady principal required strict supervision of these male callers who had to be escorted between the main gate and the clubhouse by their hostesses. Apparently, the lack of a suitable site for meeting young men had been a constant concern for the maids and their student supporters.

Typically, well over a hundred students participated in the Good Fellowship committees, and by 1929, about half of the college servants were involved in the club. The club received considerable publicity at the time of its opening and was described as the only one of its kind for women working at any large institution in the country.[135] This particular quality of social concern reflects one of Vassar's enduring traditions: the desire to create a sense of community among all of its constituencies.

Notes

Foreword

1. Letter of Matthew Vassar to President Raymond, September 1866.

Introduction

1. See Elizabeth Daniels and Clyde Griffen, *Full Steam Ahead in Poughkeepsie* (Poughkeepsie: Vassar College, 2000) for a full discussion of Vassar's transformation into a coeducational institution.
2. Elizabeth Haight, ed., *The Autobiography and Letters of Matthew Vassar* (New York: Oxford University Press, 1916), 3.
3. Dorothy Plum and George B. Dowell, *The Great Experiment: A Chronicle of Vassar* (Poughkeepsie: Vassar College, 1961), 5.
4. Benson Lossing, *The Vassar Campus 1861–1921* (New York: C. A. Alvord, 1867), 3–4.
5. In 1866 the word "female" was dropped from the college's name following a public campaign by Sarah Hale, editor of *Godey's Lady's Book*, who considered the term vulgar. Sarah Hale, "Vassar College," *Godey's Lady's Book* 73 (August 1866): 170.
6. Plum and Dowell, *The Great Experiment*, 7.
7. Haight, *The Autobiography*, 76–77.
8. Ibid., 42.
9. Matthew Vassar, *Historical Sketch of Vassar College* (New York: S. W. Green, 1876), 9.
10. Frances Ann Wood, *Earliest Years at Vassar* (Poughkeepsie: Vassar College, 1909), 6.
11. Paul Turner, *Campus* (New York: Architectural History Foundation, 1984), 47.
12. Ibid., 140, and Helen L. Horowitz, "The Design of Women's Higher Education; The Architecture and Landscapes of Women's Colleges in the United States," in *The Wise Woman Buildeth Her House*, Margrith Wilke et al., eds. (Groningen: RUG, Werkgroep Vrouwenstudies Letteren, 1992), 19–20.
13. Helen Horowitz, *Alma Mater*, 2nd ed. (Amherst: University of Massachusetts Press, 1993), 20–22.
14. Ibid., 20–21.
15. Sarah Hale, "Vassar College to be Opened this Year," *Godey's Lady's Book* 68. (January 1864): 94.
16. Margaret Birney Vickery, *Buildings for Bluestockings* (Newark: University of Delaware Press, 1999), 128–30.
17. Haight, *Autobiography,* 65.
18. Cited in Elizabeth Daniels, *From Main to Mudd* (Poughkeepsie: Vassar College, 1987), 21.
19. Vassar, *Historical Sketch*, 8.
20. John Howard Raymond, *Vassar College* (New York: S. W. Green, 1873), 13.
21. Ibid., 35.
22. Horowitz, *Alma Mater*, 61.
23. Ida Treat, "Vassar," *Town and Country* 114 (August 1960): pp. 86-93 and p. 111.
24. Horowitz, *Alma Mater*, 63–64.
25. Ibid., 62–63.
26. James Monroe Taylor and Elizabeth Hazelton Haight, *Vassar* (New York: Oxford University Press, 1915), 125–28.
27. Haight, *Autobiography,* 5.
28. Ibid., 125.
29. John Raymond, *Vassar College* (New York: S. W. Green, 1873), 28–31.
30. Taylor and Haight, *Vassar*, 138–42.
31. Ibid., Chapters 6–7.
32. Horowitz, *Alma Mater*, 91.
33. Ibid., Chapter 6.
34. Ibid., 83.
35. Taylor and Haight, *Vassar*, 156–61.
36. Statement of Appreciation from Trustees to Charles Collens, n.d., box 16, folder 22, Henry Noble MacCracken Papers Archives and Special Collections Papers, Vassar College (hereafter cited as HNM).

37. Philip Sawyer, "Early Days of York & Sawyer," *Journal of the American Institute of Architects* 16 (November 1951): 198.

38. See James Monroe Taylor, "Vassar's Contribution to Educational Theory and Practice," in *The Fiftieth Anniversary of the Opening of Vassar College A Record* (Poughkeepsie: Vassar College, 1916), 41–43.

39. See Taylor, *Vassar*, 153–55, and Elizabeth Daniels, *Bridges to the World* (Poughkeepsie: College Avenue Press, 1994), 105–107 for a more detailed discussion of this issue.

40. Horowitz, *Alma Mater*, 222.

41. MacCracken, *The Hickory Limb* (New York: Charles Scribner's Sons, 1950), 29.

42. For a more complete discussion of his life, see his autobiography, *The Hickory Limb* and Elizabeth Daniels' biography of MacCracken, *Bridges*.

43. Board of Trustees Minutes, 1945/6, p. 9, Vassar Special Collections.

44. Daniels, *Bridges*, 107–10.

45. Jean Ellis Poletti, "A Liberal Education, 1936," *Vassar Alumnae Magazine* 21, no. 7 (July 1936): 4.

46. Daniels, *Bridges*, 118–19.

47. MacCracken, *The Hickory Limb*, 117.

48. See Ellen Swallow Richards, *Euthenics*, 2nd ed. (Boston: Thomas Todd, 1912) for a complete discussion of this field.

49. Ibid., ix.

50. Julia Lathrop, "The Highest Education for Women," in *The Fiftieth Anniversary of the Opening of Vassar College A Record* (Poughkeepsie: Vassar College, 1916), 81–95.

51. Lathrop, "The Highest Education for Women," 92.

52. MacCracken, *Hickory Limb*, 27.

53. Ibid., 26.

54. Report on the Proposed Grouping of Studies within the Field of Euthenics, February 1926, box 4, folder 46, HNM.

55. Press release, 9 June 1924, box 69, folder 45, HNM.

56. Building and Grounds 1915–49, n.d., box 16, folder 42, HNM.

57. Plum and Dowell, *The Great Experiment*, 39, 81.

58. "A Tribute to Henry Noble MacCracken President of Vassar College, 1915–1946," *Vassar Quarterly* 55 (June 1970): 37.

59. *Vassar Alumnae Magazine* 49 (June 1964).

60. Ibid., 5.

61. Ibid.

62. Ibid.

63. "Vassar's Rank," Vassar's *Newsletter* vol. VI, no. 2 (February 1963), Vassar's Office of Public Relations.

64. Daniels and Griffen, *Full Steam Ahead*, 17.

65. Board of Trustees Minutes, minutes box 1 1933–1974/5, of 5, Vassar Special Collections.

66. Daniels and Griffen, *Full Steam Ahead*, 17.

67. Georgette Weir, "Remembering Alan Simpson," *Vassar Quarterly* 94 (Fall 1998): 15.

68. Robert DeMaria, Maurice F. Edelson, and Frances Prindle Taft, "A Tribute to Virginia B. Smith," *Vassar Quarterly* 82 (Fall 1986): 2.

69. *Vassar Views* 122 (May 1997): 1.

70. Ibid., 1–2.

71. *Vassar Views* 122 (May 1997): 7

From Racetrack to Academic Park

1. "Schools of Tomorrow," *Time Magazine* vol. 76, no. 11 (12 September 1960): 74

2. James Monroe Taylor, "The Vassar Campus: A History 1861–1914," *Vassar Quarterly* 1 (July 1916): 173.

3. Vassar, *Historical Sketch*, 7.

4. Andrew Jackson Downing, *A Treatise on the Theory and Practice of Landscape Gardening*, 6th ed., (New York: A. O. Moore & Company, 1859), 53.

5. Rosalie Thornton McKenna, "A Study of the Architecture of the Main Building and the Landscaping of Vassar College, 1860–70" (MA Thesis, Vassar College, 1949), 133.

6. Ibid., 134.

7. Robert Clarke, *Ellen Swallow, The Woman Who Founded Ecology,* (Chicago: Follett Publishing Company, 1973), 152.

8. Dorothy A. Plum and George B. Plum, *The Magnificent Enterprise, A Chronicle of Vassar College* (Poughkeepsie: Vassar College, 1961), 57.

9. Ibid., 119.

10. MacCracken, *The Hickory Limb*, 122.

11. Diana Balmori, Diane Kostial McGuire, and Eleanor M. McPeck, *Beatrix Farrand's American Landscapes, Her Gardens and Campuses* (Sagaponack, New York: Sagapress,Inc., 1985), 179-80.

12. H. N. MacCracken, "Conservation of the American Landscape," *Vassar Quarterly* 14 (June 1939): 21–22.

13. Alan Simpson, "'The River': A Case Study in Man's Relation to His Environment," *Vassar Alumnae Magazine* 51 (April 1966): 9.

14. MacCracken, *The Hickory Limb*, 122

Walks

1. For a detailed history of Main Building see Rosalie Thornton McKenna, "A Study of the Architecture of the Main Building & the Landscaping of Vassar College 1860–70," (MA Thesis, Vassar College, 1949).

2. Adolf K. Placzek, *Macmillan Encyclopedia* Vol. 4 (New York: Free Press, 1982), 189.

3. Ibid., 541–49.

4. McKenna, "A Study," 7.

5. Ibid., 31.

6. Ibid., chapter XI.

7. Letter from Harmon H. Goldstone to James J. Heslin, director of the New York Historical Society, 19 January 1982, Vassar College Archives and Special Collections, Vassar College Library (hereafter cited as VACSC).

8. Plum and Dowell, *The Great Experiment*, 24.

9. Taylor and Haight, *Vassar*, 172.

10. Brochure, AAUW House Tour, 15 May 1971, Vassariana, box 6, folder 38, VACSC.

11. Press release, n.d., Vassariana, box 6, file 81, VACSC.

12. Vassar, *Historical Sketch*, 16.

13. John Hupcey, Vassar College Chapel, pamphlet, February 1983, box 6, folder 49, VACSC.

14. Richard Joncas, David Newman, and Paul V. Turner, *Stanford University* (New York: Princeton Architectural Press, 1999).

15. Bernice Lippitt Thomas, "Campus Angels" *Vassar Quarterly* vol. 99, no. 1 (Winter 2002): 15.

16. Hupcey, Vassar College Chapel, np.

17. MacCracken, *Hickory Limb*, 29.

18. John Morris Dixon, *Progressive Architecture* vol. 75, no. 3 (March 1995): 68.

19. Michael J., Crosbie, *Cesar Pelli Selected and Current work* (Victoria, Australia: The Images Publishing Group Pty Ltd, 1993), 11.

20. John Pastier, *Cesar Pelli Buildings and Projects 1965–90* (New York: Rizzoli International, 1990), 19.

21. Georges Teyssot, ed., *The American Lawn* (New York: Princeton Architectural Press,1999).

22. Miss Avery's Will, n.d., box 18, folder 7, HNM.

23. Letter from McCracken to Avery, 15 January 1926, ibid.

24. Memo, 20 September 1926, "furnishings" file, Vassar, Main Basement Files.

25. Memo, 7 December 1925, ibid.

26. Memo, 15 February 1927, "costs" folder, Vassar, Main Basement Files.

27. Andrea Pawlyna, "Meeting Set on State Order to Desegregate Black Dorm at Vassar," *Poughkeepsie Journal*, 7 November 1974, 4.

28. McKenna, "A Study," 32.

29. Elizabeth Hazelton Haight, "Taylor Hall: The New Art Building at Vassar College,"*Art and Archaeology* 2 (July–December 1915): 54–57.

30. Pamela Askew, "The Department of Art at Vassar: 1865–1931," in *The Early Years of Art History in the United States,* ed. Craig Hugh Smyth and Peter M. Lukehart (Princeton: Department of Art and Archaeology, 1993), 57–63.

31. Vassar, *Historical Sketch*, 16.

32. Fanny Borden, "Vassar College Library Building," *Vassar Alumnae Magazine* vol. 23, no. 1 (15 October 1937): 3.

33. Borden, "Vassar College," 3.

34. "Announcing a New Building," *Vassar College Alumnae Magazine* vol. 21, no. 1 (October 1935): 10.

35. Agnes Rindge, "The Art Department in New Quarters," *Vassar Alumnae Magazine* vol. 23, no. 6 (June 1938): 3–9.

36. Elizabeth A. Daniels, *Main to Mudd, and More* (Poughkeepsie: Vassar College, 1996), 36.

37. Philip Sawyer, "Early Days of York and Sawyer," *Journal of the American Institute of Architects* 16 (November 1951): 195–200.

38. Daniels, *From Main to Mudd*, 36.

39. Henry Noble MacCracken, "President's Conception of Alumnae House," Alumnae House, pamphlet, 8 May 1923, VACSC.

40. Plum and Dowell, *The Great Experiment*, 46–47.

41. MacCracken, "President's Conception."

42. Olivia Josselyn Hall, pamphlet, November 1912, box 6, folder 56, VACSC.

43. "Girls Happiest in Josselyn Hall," n.d., VACSC, box 6, folder 56.

44. Olivia Josselyn Hall, pamphlet.

45. Horowitz, *Alma Mater*, 93–94.

46. Ibid., 93.

47. Fanny Cohen and Elizabeth Boyd, *Vassar* (New York: Chasmar Press, 1896), 23.

48. Taylor and Haight, *Vassar*, 175.

49. Plum and Dowell, *Magnificent Enterprise*, 31.

50. Ibid., 39.

51. Ibid., 37.

52. Ibid., 39.

53. Plum and Dowell, *Magnificent Enterprise*, 44.

54. Joseph Herendon Clark, *Autobiography of an Architect* (Portola California: self-published, 1974), 57. Also cited by Daniels, *Main to Mudd*, 47.

55. "Auditorium Building, Vassar College," *The Brickbuilder* vol. 22 no. 11 (November 1913): 161–64.

56. Daniels, *Main to Mudd*, 49.

57. News From Vassar, press release, 12 May 1973, box 6, folder 87, VACSC.

58. Plum and Dowell, *The Great Experiment*, 24.

59. Allan Tempko, *Eero Saarinen* (New York: George Braziller, 1962): 14.

60. Masato Oishi (ed.) *Eero Saarinen* (Tokyo, Japan: A+U Publishing Co., 1984), 191–97.

61. Aline B.Louchheim, "Now Saarinen the Son," *New York Times Magazine,* 26 April 1953, 26.

62. Letter from Keene Richards to MacCracken, 16 April 1928, Cushing Hall files, Vassar Main Basement Files.

63. Cushing Hall Vassar College, fundraising brochure, n.d., box 6, folder 52 VACSC.

64. Report to Committee on New Dormitory Group, 4 October 1924, box 16, folder 58, HNM.

65. Unsigned letter to MacCracken, 2 February 1926, Cushing Hall, box 6, folder 52, VACSC.

66. Letter from Jean Palmer to MacCracken, 2 February 1926, box 17, folder 18, HNM.

67. Helen Kenyon Hall of Physical Education, press release, n.d., VACSC.

68. Henry Noble MacCracken, "To the Alumnae of Vassar College," Dedication of Helen Kenyon Hall of Physical Education, Semi-Annual Meeting of the Associate Alumnae of Vassar College, 22–24 February 1934, box 6, folder 58, VACSC.

69. The New Gymnasium of Vassar College, 1929, box 6, folder 59, VACSC.

70. "New Vassar Sports Building Replaces Gym that has Served College 43 Years," *Poughkeepsie Evening Star* , 10 February 1934, np.

71. Catherine Bauer, "New Calisthenium for Vassar Female College," *Arts Weekly*, 4 May 1932, 193.

72. Elizabeth I. Bauer, "Vassar Buildings," *Miscellany News*, 14 May 1932, 2, 6.

73. Minutes of Trustees Committee on Grounds, 14 December 1925, box 4, folder 55, HNM.

74. Wimpfheimer Nursery School, pamphlet, box 21, folder 9, VACSC.

75. Letter from MacCracken to Mrs. Hadley, 18 September 1926, box 5, folder 1, HNM.

76. Letter from MacCracken to Charles Collens, 18 March, 1925, box 16, folder 57, HNM.

77. Memorandum of Interview between MacCracken and Annie MacCleod, 1 October 1924, Blodgett box 6, folder 47, VACSC.

78. Blodgett Hall of Euthenics, brochure, box 16, folder 50, HNM.

79. See for example, Dorothy Schaffter, "The Study of Housing at Vassar," *Vassar Alumnae Magazine* vol. 23, no. 3 (15 January 1938): 9–10, and "The Social Museum," *Vassar Alumnae Magazine* vol. 23, no. 3 (15 January 1938): 11.

80. Henry Noble MacCracken, "Social Science Museum," *Vassar Alumnae Magazine* vol. 22, no. 5 (15 April 1937): 13.

81. Ibid.

82. Henry Noble MacCracken, "Blodgett Hall: Purpose and Fulfillment," *Alumnae Magazine* vol. 24, no. 2 (December 1938): 18.

83. Helen Drusilla Lockwood, "The Meaning of Euthenics" *Educational Record* 10 (April 1929): 71–93.

84. Notes from a motion of trustees, December 1914, box 16, folder 60, HNM

85. Haight, *Autobiography*, 97, 99–100, 106.

86. Benson Lossing, *Vassar College and its Founder* (New York: Alvord Printer, 1867): 146–50.

87. Sally Gregory Kohlstedt, "Maria Mitchell: The Advancement of Women in Science," *New England Quarterly* vol. 51 no. 1 (March 1978): 40. More detailed accounts of Mitchell's life include: Helen Wright, *Sweeper in the Sky: The Life of Maria Mitchell, First Woman Astronomer in America* (New York: McMillan, 1949), and Phebe Kendall, *Maria Mitchell, Her Life, Letters and Journals* (Boston: Lee & Shepard, 1896).

88. Kohlstedt, "Maria Mitchell," 44–45.

89. Alice Owen Albertson, "Maria Mitchell 1818–1889," *The Vassar Quarterly* vol. 7.

90. This discussion of Mitchell's teaching is based largely on Kohlstedt, "Maria Mitchell," 41–43.

91. Mary Harriott Norris, *The Golden Age of Vassar* (Poughkeepsie: Vassar College, 1915), 81–82, and Frances Wood, *Earliest Years at Vassar* (Poughkeepsie: Vassar College Press, 1909), 82–83.

92. Duane Pearson, "National Historic Landmarks Presentation Ceremony for the Vassar College Observatory," 9 December 1991, U.S. Department of the Interior, 3–4.

93. Meeting of the Alumnae Association, 11 June 1889, Vassariana, Miscellaneous Buildings, box 6, folder 42, VCASC.

94. "The New Faculty Aula," *Vassar College Alumnae Magazine* vol. 23, no. 2 (1 December 1937): 17.

95. Cohen and Boyd, *Vassar*, 25.

96. Minutes notes ,Vassariana, n.d., Vassariana, Miscellaneous Buildings, box 6, folder 42, VCASC.

97. Meeting of the Alumnae Association, June 11, 1889.

98. Cohen and Boyd, *Vassar*, 29.

99. Executive Committee, notes, 20 September 1892, Vassariana, Miscellaneous Buildings, box 6, folder 42, VCASC.

100. Executive Committee, notes, 13 November 1901, 12 February 1902, 12 March 1902, 12 June 1905, 20 June 1905, Vassariana, Miscellaneous Buildings, box 6, folder 42, VCASC, and AUTHOR, *The Vassar Campus*, 9.

101. College catalogue clipping, n.d., Vassariana, Miscellaneous Buildings, box 6, folder 41, VCASC.

102. "The New Faculty Aula,"*Vassar College Alumnae Magazine* vol. 23, no. 2 (1 December 1937).

103. MacCracken, *The Hickory Limb*, 94.

104. Plum and Dowell, *The Great Experiment*, 26.

105. Ibid., 35.

106. College catalogue clipping, n.d., Vassariana, box 6, folder 39, VCASC.

107. Barbara Stimson, "'Now it Can Be Told'*or* Inside Stories of Baldwin House," *Vassar Quarterly* vol. 26, no. 2 (December 1940): 12.

108. Ibid.

109. Stimson reports that discussions with the health department, the Buildings and Grounds Committee of the Trustees, the business manager, the president, and the students led to the following requirements for the building: 1) maximum sun and air; 2) enough single rooms for the college population; 3) modern hospital equipment; 4) fireproof construction; 5) an elevator; 6) a rock-bottom budget. Apparently, the college had been fundraising heavily for its seventy-fifth anniversary celebrations and did not want to seek a gift for the building, funding it internally instead. Dr. Stimson breezily suggests that the first requirement excluded the collegiate Gothic style; the second the colonial revival style; and three, four, and five together recommended the adoption of the modern style for the building. It is difficult to imagine a logical explanation for this set of conclusions, but in any case, they highlight the fact that the college thought it necessary to justify Baldwin's design. Better medical equipment was given priority in budgetary decisions, but Stimson mentions that "color and cheerfulness" were incorporated whenever possible in compensation for the lack of decoration. Ibid.

110. Henry Noble MacCracken, "Belle Skinner, Vassar 1887," *Vassar Quarterly* 15 (February 1930): 10–14.

111. Ibid., 12–13.
112. Ibid., 10.
113. "Skinner Memorial given to Vassar," *New York Times*, 30 November 1929, np.
114. MacCracken, "Belle Skinner," 13.
115. The Building—Its Arrangement and Equipment, pamphlet, box 6, folder 85, VCASC, 8.
116. Ellenzweig Associates, "Classroom Master Plan, Vassar College," July 1999, 12.
117. Plum and Dowell, *The Great Experiment*, 26.
118. Elizabeth Howe, "Florence Cushing," *Vassar Quarterly* vol. 13, no. 2 (March 1928): 91.
119. Aaron L. Treadwell, "The Biology Laboratory of Vassar College," reprint from the *Journal of Applied Microscopy and Laboratory Methods* 4 (1901): 1718.
120. Ibid., figs. 2–3.
121. Ibid., 1724.
122. Sanders Physics Building, box 6, folder 84, VCASC.
123. Ibid.; Taylor and Haight, *Vassar*, 126; no author, *Life at Vassar 75 Years in Pictures* (Poughkeepsie: Vassar Cooperative Bookshop, 1940), 31.
124. Lossing, *Vassar College and its Founder*, 111.
125. A detailed description of the original arrangement of the building is found in Lossing, *Vassar College and its Founder*, 154–55.
126. Ibid.
127. Vassar, *Historical Sketch of Vassar*, 22–23. A plan of the building from this time can be found on p. 22.
128. Daniels, *Main to Mudd*, 22. For a discussion of the Classical Museum in Avery see Elizabeth Hazelton Haight, "The New Classical Museum" *Vassar College Alumnae Magazine* 24 (January 1939): 13.
129. *Vassar Views* 130 (Spring 2002): 2.
130. "The Architecture of Energy," *Architectural Record* 111 (January 1952): 127.
131. Ann Thorp, "The Social Side of Domestic Service at Vassar College," *Wellesley Magazine* vol. 24, no. 4 (January 1916): 6.
132. The Good Fellowship Club of Vassar College, pamphlet, Good Fellowship Club Papers, box 3, folder 4, VCASC.
133. Thorp, "The Social Side," 6–7.
134. The Good Fellowship Club, and Annual Report of the Good Fellowship Club, 14 May 1915, Good Fellowship Papers, box 3, folder 4, VCASC provide samples of events and classes held at the club house.
135. Grace Elisabeth Paine, "The Maids' Club at Vassar College," *Good Housekeeping* (June 1913): 809–811.

Bibliography

Collections
Archives and Special Collections Department, Vassar College Library, Vassar College, Poughkeepsie, New York.
Building and Grounds Archives, Vassar College, Poughkeepsie, New York
Office of College Relations, Vassar College, Poughkeepsie, New York
Prints and Drawings, Vassar College Art Library, Vassar College, Poughkeepsie, New York
Vassar College Board, Trustee Meeting Notes, Vassar College, Poughkeepsie, New York

Vassar Periodicals
Vassar Alumnae Magazine
Vassar Miscellany
Vassar Quarterly

Allis, Jean McCoy. "Vassar Village." *Vassar Alumnae Magazine* 24 (June 1939): 6–8.
"An Architecture of Energy-Cooperative Dormitory, Vassar College." *Architectural Record* 111 (January 1952): 127–34.
"Auditorium Building Vassar College," *The Brick Builder* 22 (1913): Plates 161–64.
Bauer, Catherine. "New Calisthenium for Vassar Female College." *Arts Weekly*, 4 May 1932, 192–93.
Birketts, Gunnar. "Eero Saarinen, Interview with Gunnar Birkets." *A+U* 163 (April 1984): 224.
Boonin, Sara. "Planning and Planting a Shakespeare Garden." *Vassar Quarterly* 76 (Winter 1979): 28–30.
Candib, Dorothy. "Wanting to Know. . . Olmsted." *Vassar Quarterly* 71/72 (Summer 1975): 27–29.
Clark, Joseph Herendon. *Autobiography of an Architect.* Portola Valley, California: by the author, 1974.
Clarke, Robert. *Ellen Swallow, The Woman Who Founded Ecology.* Chicago: Follett Publishing Company, 1973.
"Clearing House." *Vassar Quarterly* (May 1929): 100–106.
Cohen, Fanny and Elizabeth Boyd, eds. *Vassar.* New York: Chasmar Press, 1896.
Collens, Charles. "Vassar College." *American Architect—Architectural Review* 123 (January 1923): 48–55.
Crosbie, Michael J. *Color & Context, The Architecture of Perry Dean Rogers &Partner.* Rockport, Massachusetts: The American Institute of Architects Press by Rockport Publishers Inc., 1995.
Daniels, Elizabeth A. *Bridges to the World.* Clinton Corners, New York: College Avenue Press, 1994.
Daniels, Elizabeth A. and Clyde Griffen. *Full Steam Ahead in Poughkeepsie.* Poughkeepsie: Vassar College, 2000.
_____. *Main to Mudd.* Poughkeepsie, New York: Vassar College, 1987.
_____. *Main to Mudd, and More.* Poughkeepsie, New York: Vassar College, 1996.
DeMaria, Robert, Maurice F. Edelson, and Frances Prindle Taft. "A Tribute to Virginia B. Smith." *Vassar Quarterly* 82 (Fall 1986): 1–2.
Dixon, John Morris. "Frances Lehman Loeb Art Center, Vassar College." *Progressive Architecture* 76 (March 1995): 68–77.
Downer, Henry E. "The Grounds at Vassar." *Vassar Quarterly* 16 (February 1931): 1–8.
Downing, Andrew Jackson. *A Treatise on the Theory and Practice of Landscape Gardening.* 6th ed. New York: A.O. Moore & Company, 1859.
Drouilhet, Elizabeth Moffatt. "Cooperative Living on the Campus." *Vassar Alumnae Magazine* (April 1943): 10–11.
Fergusson, Frances Daly. "The Ferment and True Discourse of Diversity—Inaugural Address." *Vassar Quarterly* 83 (Winter 1986): 11–12.
Gutman, Thea. "Introducing Virginia Smith." *Vassar Quarterly* 73/74 (Summer 1977): 7–12.

Hale, Sarah Josepha. "Vassar College, The New Plan of Organization Examined: Only 'One Defect' and This May Be Easily Remedied." *Godey's Lady's Book* 68 (February 1864): 199–200.

_____. "Vassar Female College." *Godey's Lady's Book* 63 (October 1861): 347–48.

Halsted, Carolyn. "College Life at Vassar and Wellesley." *Metropolitan Magazine* 8 (July 1898): 37–48.

Herman, Debra. "College and After: The Vassar Experiment in Women's Education, 1861–1924." PhD Dissertation, Stanford University, 1979.

Horowitz, Helen Lefkowitz. *Alma Mater.* 2nd ed. Amherst: University of Massachusetts Press, 1993.

Jordy, William H. *American Buildings and Their Architect.* Vol. 5, *The Impact of European Modernism in the Mid-Twentieth Century.* New York: Oxford University Press, 1972.

Kendall, Phoebe. *Maria Mitchell, Her Life, Letters and Journals.* Boston: Lee and Shepard, 1896.

Kohlstedt, Sally Gregory. "Maria Mitchell: The Advancement of Women in Science." *New England Quarterly* 51 (March 1978): 39–63.

Linn, Charles. "Students Stare Down The Stars At Vassar's New Observatory." *Architectural Record* 186 (February 1998): 112–13.

Lockwood, Helen. "The Meaning of Euthenics." *Educational Record* (April 1929).

Lossing, Benson. *Vassar College and its Founder.* New York: Alvord Printer, 1867.

MacCracken, Henry Noble. "Belle Skinner, Vassar 1887." *Vassar Quarterly* (Feb 1930).

_____. "Blodgett Hall: Purpose and Fulfillment." *Vassar Alumnae Magazine* 24 (Dec 1938): 18.

_____. "Conservation of the American Landscape." *Vassar Quarterly* 24 (June 1939): 21–22.

_____. *The Hickory Limb.* New York: Charles Scribner & Sons, 1950.

_____. "Social Science Museum." *Vassar Alumnae Magazine* 22 (15 April 1937): 13.

_____. "Three Decades at Vassar." *Vassar Alumnae Magazine* 29 (June 1945): 3, 11.

Massello, David. *Architecture Without Rules.* New York: W. W. Norton & Company, 1993.

Mays, Vernon. "Uses of Glass." *Progressive Architecture* 70 (March 1989): 106–111.

McClelland, Nancy V. "College Life at Vassar." *The National Magazine* 7 (October 1897): 3–12.

McFarland, Jean H. "The New Library." *Vassar Quarterly* 49 (December 1963): 8–11.

McKenna, Rosalie Thornton. "A Study of the Architecture of the Main Building & the Landscaping of Vassar College 1860–70." MA Thesis, Vassar College, 1949.

"New Faculty Aula." *Vassar Alumnae Magazine* 23 (December 1937): 17.

"Newest Note in the Heterogenesis of Vassar." *Architectural Record* 126 (September 1959): 193–85.

Oishi, Masato, ed. *Eero Saarinen.* Tokyo: Architecture and Urbanism, 1984.

"Organic Chemistry: Seeley G. Mudd Chemistry Building, Vassar College." *Architectural Record* 174 (March 1986): 136–45.

Palmer, Barbara Heslan. "Lace Bonnets and Academic Gowns: Faculty Development in Four Women's Colleges, 1875–1915." PhD Dissertation, Boston College, 1980.

Pearson, Clifford. "Admission House Vassar College, Poughkeepsie, New York." *Architectural Record* 186 (February 1998): 134–36.

Pearson, Duane. National Historic Landmarks Presentation Ceremony for the Vassar College Observatory, 9 December 1991, United States Department of the Interior, National Park Service, Hyde Park, New York.

Placzek, Adolf K., ed. *Macmillan Encyclopedia of Architects.* New York: Free Press, 1982.

Plum, Dorothy A, and George B. Plum. *The Magnificent Enterprise, A Chronicle of Vassar College.* Poughkeepsie, New York: Vassar College, 1961.

"Portrait." *Progressive Architecture* 27 (December 1946): 14.

Raymond, John Howard. *Vassar College.* New York: S. W. Green, 1873.

"Remembering." *Vassar Quarterly* 94 (Fall 1998): 14.

Richards, Ellen Swallow. *Euthenics*, 2nd ed. Boston: Thomas Todd, 1912.

Roberts, Edith A. and Elsa Rehmann. *American Plants for American Gardens.* New York: MacMillan Company, 1929.

Rodman, Nancy G. "Vassar Buildings." *Miscellany News*, 14 May 1932.

Sawyer, Philip. "Early Days of York and Sawyer." *Journal of American Institute of Architects* 16 (November 1951): 195–200.

Schmertz, Mildred F. "'Recycling Main'—A Landmark at Vassar." *Architectural Record* 162 (July 1977): 73–78.

Schuyler, Montgomery. "Architecture of American Colleges, Three Women's Colleges—Vassar, Wellesley and Smith." *Architectural Record* (1912): 513–537.

Simpson, Alan. "Inaugural Address." *Vassar Quarterly* 50 (December 1964): 13–15.

_____. "A New Approach Through Environmental Studies." *Vassar Quarterly* 51/52 (April 1966): 4–8.

_____. "An Open Letter to the Alumnae." *Vassar Quarterly* 52 (February 1967): 2–3.

_____. "'The River': A Case Study in Man's Relation to His Environment." *Vassar Alumnae Magazine* 51 (April 1966): 9–11.

"Situation Called For An Arc-Like Plan." *Architectural Record* 126 (September 1959): 168–70.

"Skinner Memorial Given to Vassar." *New York Times*, 30 November 1929.

Staz, Clarice. *The Rockefeller Women.* New York: St.Martin's Press, 1995.

Stimson, Barbara B. "'Now It Can be Told' Inside Stories of Baldwin House." *Vassar Quarterly* 26 (December 1940): 12–13.

Sullivan, Patrick H. "Omnium Gathering." *Vassar Quarterly* 79/80 (Fall 82): 4.

Taylor, James Monroe. "The Vassar Campus; A History 1886–1914." *Vassar Quarterly* 1 (July 1916): 159–73.

Taylor, James Monroe and Elizabeth Hazelton Haight. *Vassar.* New York: Oxford University Press, 1915.

Temko, Allan. *Eero Saarinen.* New York: Braziller, 1962.

Treadle, Aaron. "The Biology Laboratory of Vassar College," *Journal of Applied Microscopy and Laboratory Methods* 4 (DATE?): 1717–1725.

"Tribute to Henry Noble MacCracken President of Vassar College, 1915–46." *Vassar Quarterly* 55 (June 1970): 37.

"Tribute to Sarah Gibson Blanding." *Vassar Alumnae Magazine* 49 (June 1964): 4–15.

Turner, Paul Venable. *Campus, An American Planning Tradition.* Cambridge: MIT Press, 1984.

Underwood, Loring. *The Garden and its Accessories.* Boston: Little, Brown and Company, 1907.

"Vassar College Library Building," *Vassar Alumnae Magazine* 23 (October 15, 1937): 3–7.

Vassar, Matthew. *The Autobiography and Letters of Matthew Vassar.* Edited by Elizabeth Hazelton Haight. New York: OUP, 1916.

_____. *Historical Sketch of Vassar College.* New York: S. W. Green, 1876.

Washburn, Margaret Floy. "The Vassar Golf Course." *Vassar Quarterly* 16 (November 1931): 268–73.

Williamson, Jr. George. "Class Trees as Totems." *Vassar Quarterly* 75/76: 34.

Withey, Henry F. and Elsie Rathburn Withey. *Biographical Dictionary of American Architects-Deceased.* Los Angeles: New Age Publishing Company, 1956.

Wright, Margaret R. "From Hygiene to Politics of Ecology: A History of Environmental Science at Vassar College." *Vassar Quarterly* 90 (Fall 1994): 18–21.

York, Content. "The College Girl's Room." *House Beautiful* (October 1916): 278–280.

Yudkin, Marcia. "Earth, Air, Wind, Hearth: The Woman Who Founded Ecology." *Vassar Quarterly* 77/78 (Spring 1982): 32–34.